Dee
Secure
Cared For
Significant   *Successful*

Show him I love him   help him to be
successful

Grace to Relate

Seeing Relationships in a New Light

Dr. Scott E. Hadden

This book is dedicated to my wife Pamela,
who has inspired me, been patient with me,
loved me, and stood by me all these years.
I love you!

Contents

Acknowledgments

In particular I would like to acknowledge Theron Messer, whose friendship and guidance helped me produce this material. His encouragement and insights helped make it possible for me to continue. Theron passed into glory in June 2014.

I also would like to acknowledge my Scope Ministries International staffers, whose passion for the Lord and insights into relationships have been invaluable. In particular I would like to thank Sandra Pickard, Rick and Lori Fry, Darrell Gallear, and Kandi Taylor, whose editing and critiques helped make this material a reality. Many thanks to Bruce Barteaux, whose teaching on oneness is an essential base for relationships.

Introduction

With a weary sigh, she slowly eased herself down and sat on a grassy slope that overlooked the sea. She didn't live far from the shore, but the journey had been a difficult one. She was so tired, and everything took effort. People scurried past her, like water tripping past a stone, all hurrying toward the shore. The teacher from Nazareth was there, and everyone had heard of him. Some were saying He was a great teacher, but many others were saying He was more than that. They said He could perform miracles.

And He could heal.

She rested a few moments more, then slowly pushed herself up and followed the crowd. If only she could get near Him. If only…People continued to push their way past her, eager to get closer. She craned her neck to catch sight of Him, but the crowds were pressing in so that she could hardly see Him now. Tears filled her eyes.

This wretched illness. For twelve years she had been hemorrhaging, and none of the many physicians she had gone to had done anything for it. They eagerly took her money, made all sorts of grand promises, and then produced nothing. Some had even made her worse, and always the treatments were torturously painful. Now she had nothing.

Nothing, of course, but this wretched illness.

Slowly, she walked across the beach to the edge of the crowd. She could just see Him now, still standing by the edge of the shore, His disciples nearby, and the boat in which He had arrived pulled up onto the sand.

Just then she heard a loud commotion as a man shoved his way through the throng, bustling past her toward Jesus. The crowd parted slightly at his urgent insisting and out of respect for his title. She recognized the man as Jairus, a synagogue official. Once Jairus reached the teacher, he threw himself down at His feet and announced that his daughter was sickend to the point of death. "Please come and lay your hands on her," he begged Jesus, "that she may get well and live."

In dismay, the woman watched as the teacher agreed and followed Jairus. The tears again welled up in her eyes. She would never reach Him now. She could never have gotten through the crowds anyway, and besides, a poor old woman was nothing compared with a synagogue official. What were her needs in contrast to those of someone so important?

Weary, she watched the two men climb back up the shore away from the beach, the crowd still pressing in as closely as ever. As they edged nearer, an idea came to her. As soon as she could, she decided, she would touch him. The power of such a man surely touched everything about Him, even the clothes He wore. She wouldn't have to bother Him. She would just touch Him once; He would never notice.

"If I just touch His garments," she told herself, "I shall get well."

Finally Jesus and Jairus walked near her. Mustering all the strength she had, she threw herself into the throng, pushing her way through until she came close enough to touch him. With a trembling hand she quickly reached out and touched the hem of His cloak.

Like a bolt of lightning, the power surged through her body, and the weakness that had hung so heavily for so long evaporated as if it had never been there at all. Immediately she felt lighter, and for the first time in years she stood up straight, taking a deep breath.

She smiled at His retreating back and then turned to go, certain she'd leave unnoticed. But she heard a quiet yet powerful voice ask, "Who touched my garments?"

The woman froze in fear. Behind her, she heard the men who traveled with Him, His disciples, comment on the large crowd around Jesus. "Look at the multitude pressing in on you," they said. "What do you mean 'Who touched me'?"

Despite their protestations, He was staring straight at her; she could feel it. She turned around and faced Him, looking Him squarely in the eyes. His expression seared her, and in an instant she realized He knew who she was and that she had touched His cloak.

Shaking with fear, she fell down before Him.

"I touched your cloak, sir," she said timidly. "I meant you no harm. I've been sick for so long, and I thought that if I just touched your garments, I would be made well, so that's what I did." She pressed her forehead deep into the sand, terrified of what He might do. After all, this was no ordinary prophet. This man had the power of God at His fingertips. Surely He would be angry with her for stealing power from Him, and who knew what He might do?

She waited in silence for His wrath, but it never came. Slowly she looked up and gasped in surprise, for He stared at her not in anger, but in love, greater love than she had ever before experienced.

"Daughter," He replied gently, "your faith has made you well. Go in peace, and be healed of your affliction."

We don't know her name, but we know her story. She risked everything to touch His garment. Can you imagine how a Pharisee would react if a woman had touched his garment? She could have been rebuked, rejected, and shamed had Jesus been like any other religious leader.

Yet she risked it all on the man named Jesus. She touched His garment and experienced not only a healing but a much-greater surprise.

She already knew she would be healed if only she could just touch the garments, so what was this life-changing surprise?

Let's look at the story again, in Mark 5:31–34: *And His disciples said to Him, "You see the crowd pressing in on you, and you say, 'Who touched Me?'" And He looked around to see the woman who had done this. But the woman, fearing and trembling, aware of what had happened to her, came and fell down before Him and told Him the whole truth. And He said to her, "Daughter, your faith has made you well; go in peace, and be healed of your affliction."*

The woman, fearful and shaken, fell down before Christ. She had been caught and would have to pay the price. How did Jesus respond to the woman? Jesus gently gave her His blessing, "Go in peace, and be healed." All she thought she knew about "holy" untouchable men was dashed. Here was a man who cared, a holy man with compassion. She knew this Jesus came from God, but she wasn't ready for His response. She did not expect it. God cares and is gentle. There was (and is) no reason for fear. Imagine that! She would never be the same. In seeing His compassion, her passion for God was unleashed.

There you have it—one "little" experience with God and a life changes. One moment of grace changed the heart of an "unclean" woman. This woman had begun a relationship with the God of the universe. Did I mention that she was healed?

This is a book about the healing of relationships. In the next few chapters we will see that fulfilling earthly relationships begin with an intimate heavenly relationship. This relationship with God forms the basis of healthy relationships with our fellow people.

Chapter One

Getting to Know You

I'm not one who loves musicals, but occasionally a certain song sticks in my head. So when I think about relationships, the lyrics of "Getting to Know You," a show tune from Rodgers and Hammerstein's production *The King and I,* bounces around my mind. Listen with me:

Getting to know you
Getting to feel free and easy
When I am with you
Getting to know what to say

The first priority of a graceful relationship is getting to know each other. As you grow in your knowledge of a person, you grow in love for that person. Remember what Jesus said to His disciples in John 14:21: *He who has my commandments and keeps them is the one who loves me; and he who loves me will be loved by my Father, and I will love him and will disclose myself to him.*

Notice that knowing God and walking in His way are intimately connected—so intimate, in fact, that the word "love" comes into play. Love results in the disclosure of Christ. Now an interesting event occurs: The more you know Him, the more you love Him and know He loves you. The more you know He loves you, the more He reveals Himself to you. On and on it goes. Sort of like Jimi Hendrix getting guitar feedback from his amplifier while playing "The Star-Spangled Banner" at Woodstock in 1969, only better.

So how important is love in relationships? In Matthew 22:35–40, we read, *One of them, a lawyer, asked Him a question, testing Him, "Teacher, which is the great commandment in the Law?" And He said to him, "You shall love the Lord your God with all your heart, and with all your soul, and with all your mind." This is the great and foremost commandment. The second is like it, "You shall love your neighbor as yourself." On these two commandments depend the whole Law and the Prophets.*

Loving God is so important that Jesus considered it the number-one commandment. How is it that God would command us to love Him and others?

In describing the main purpose of our relationship to God, biblical counselor Bruce Barteaux puts it this way in the class syllabus *Graceful Marriages* (Scope Ministries International):

> In the same way, through new birth, Christians now possess the Father's "DNA." We have a new human spirit that is holy, like our Father's. Since we have God the Holy Spirit in us, joined to us forever, we have oneness in nature: *I will ask the Father, and He will give you another helper, that He may be with you forever; that is the Spirit of truth, whom the world cannot receive, because it does not see Him or know Him, but you know Him because He abides with you and will be in you* (John 14:16–17).

While we already have the Holy Spirit, we are in the process of becoming like Him. We find this oneness through **practice**, which we develop through being in His **presence**. In the following passage, the apostle Paul describes how we change as we see Christ in His glory: *But we all, with unveiled face, beholding as in a mirror the glory of the Lord, are being transformed into the same image from glory to glory, just as from the Lord, the Spirit* (2 Cor. 3:18).

Our oneness with God (presence) in our spirit yearns for relationship and oneness with God in practice. So why is this so important in relationships?

Love and Oneness with God Is the Source of Oneness with Others

God created us like Himself and intended us to experience an unbroken relationship with Him. In this relationship we experience eternal life. His life in us provides the source of everything we need for life and godliness. Once we were separated from God, but God in Christ reconciled us to Himself. Once reconciled to God by faith and the indwelling Holy Spirit, we can experience life and relationships as God intended, through oneness with Him and others. Oneness with God facilitates oneness with others. Being one with God does not mean that you are God. In the same way, being one with your spouse does not mean you are your spouse.

God, by His creative work, formed Adam and Eve as His children, and by design they resembled Him through intimate association—*oneness.*

God designed us after His own nature, to multiply out of a union, a oneness. As we see in Hebrews 1, the Father made the world through the Son. And in Genesis 1, we also see the Spirit moving over the face of the deep. All three—Father, Son, and Spirit—took part in creation and worked in perfect oneness, deferring to one another. In the same manner, all that we can create would be impossible without oneness.

The creation of a new physical life requires physical oneness. If you marriage is to thrive, it needs oneness of the soul (mind, will, and emotions). Most important is the need for spiritual oneness. Oneness with God creates all that is good, for only God is good, as seen in Mark 10:18: *And Jesus said to him, "Why do you call me good? No one is good except God alone."* God's Spirit in us gives life to our spirit, and only from Him and through Him we receive what is good and do what is good, as stated in John 15:5: *I am the vine, you are the branches; he who abides in me and I in him, he bears much fruit, for apart from me you can do nothing.* God never meant for man to be alone. He created Adam and Eve to be one with Him, and as one with God, they were one with each other.

Think on these verses for a few minutes:

Then God said, "Let us make man in our image, according to our likeness" (Gen. 1:26)

For those whom He foreknew, He also predestined to become conformed to the image of His Son (Rom. 8:29)

That they may all be one; even as you, Father, are in me and I in you, that they also may be in us, so that the world may believe that you sent me (John 17:21).

Oneness in His image? Wow, what a goal! How does one even begin to comprehend, much less explain? Simply put, becoming like Him, being conformed to Him, and being one with Him are God-sized tasks! Jesus put it this way in Luke 18:27: *"The things that are impossible with people are possible with God."*

Without Him, we can achieve neither oneness nor conformity with His image. Fortunately, new birth has provided the means and ability through His life. John 3:16 is often quoted to demonstrate God's forgiveness of sins: *For God so loved the world, that He gave His only begotten Son, that whoever believes in Him shall not perish, but have eternal life.*

There is only one problem with this. The verse doesn't directly address forgiveness of sins. It's implied. What does the verse talk about? New life, eternal life, everlasting life! In spirit God has already made us conformed to His eternal image. His Spirit and man's spirit are one. He put His life within the believer. Ezekiel 36:26–27 intimates that in the new covenant, *I will give you a new heart and put a new spirit within you; and I will remove the heart of stone from your flesh and give you a heart of flesh. I will put my Spirit within you and cause you to walk in my statutes, and you will be careful to observe my ordinances."*

Our new heart and new spirit already conform to the image of Christ, as He has already made us one with Him! As believers we grow into what is already true of us. For example, there are certain things most humans do: walk upright, talk, breathe air, and so on. Newborn babies do not walk upright or talk, but they are humans who will someday grow into walking and talking. The world system believes your growth determines your being—your existence, your worth, and your value. Some grow into accountants, pastors, farmers, lawyers, or secretaries, and thus gain a sense of worth and value. Yet you do not grow into nature; you reveal it.

The worldly tendency is to attempt to gain worth and value from what you accomplish with your life. Can you imagine a new mother looking at her newborn and saying, "I wonder what she will grow up to be—a cat, a dog, or perhaps a butterfly?" Birth always determines nature. It does not determine vocation. A cat is born a cat. A human is born a human. A child of God is born a child of God. When a person is born again spiritually, the revelation of their true nature begins.

Without the knowledge of our creation in the image of God and one of our unity with Him through Christ, the search is on to "become" someone. The good news is that we *are* someone! As a result of being one with Him, we have a need for intimacy with Him. He answers our deepest longings. We have a God-shaped void that only He can fill. As His children we have His seed implanted in us and we are born from above.

In summary, God designed us to be one with Him and one with our mate. Three in one—spirit, soul, and body. We are one with God, but we are not God. Likewise we are one with our spouse, but we are not our spouse! My wife and I are one, but we don't have the same blood type!

I hope by now you see that getting to know God, or even *wanting* to know God, springs from within. His children desire to know Him intimately. We received that love for Him at the point of salvation. Do you know you already love God? When my wife and I married, we thought we loved each other immensely, but thirty-five years later we realize we barely knew what love was back then. In the same way, our love for God grows through time. We build on a foundation of love placed within us through the Holy Spirit.

Back to Matthew 22:36–40, we see that not only are we commanded to love God but to love others as we love ourselves. Therefore if you do *not* love yourself, you cannot love others! That's why it is so important to understand and receive God's love. His love for us sets us free to love others. He gives the ability to love others through His Spirit.

So see that it is…
Getting to know you—God
Getting to know you—Self
Getting to know you—Others

Getting to know You [Lord]
Getting to feel free and easy
When I am with You
Getting to know what to say

Matthew 22:36–40

"Teacher, which is the great commandment in the Law?" And He said to him, "YOU SHALL LOVE THE LORD YOUR GOD WITH ALL YOUR HEART, AND WITH ALL YOUR SOUL, AND WITH ALL YOUR MIND." This is the great and foremost commandment. The second is like it, "YOU SHALL LOVE YOUR NEIGHBOR AS YOURSELF." On these two commandments depend the whole Law and the Prophets.

Chapter Two

What Does It Take to Know Someone?

Time

A "getting to know you" relationship or marriage might continue upward of about sixty years. In 1 Peter 3:7 the Bible suggests this to husbands: *Live with your wives in an **understanding** way* [emphasis added]. This could mean that it takes longer than sixty years!

Pastoral author Andrew Farley likes to say that the Lord has us on an eighty-year plan of learning to know Him. It takes time to learn His ways, learn His thoughts, enjoy His presence, see Him deliver, see His work in others, and understand His wisdom. Getting to know God is not a race to gain information but an ongoing process of relating to Him.

Relationships begin to break down once we think we've learned all we need to know about another person and feel we've experienced everything there is to experience with another. Time is critical in developing a relationship.

We experience time in a linear fashion. We have a past, present, and future. Relationships always occur in the present, which develops from a past. The quality of the present relationship often determines its future. The perceived past and present characteristics of the relationship either give us hope or fear of its future. As we see God's great love, grace, holiness, and forgiveness, over time we gain hope that is steadfast and secure. Hebrews 6:19: *"This hope we have as an anchor of the soul, a hope both sure and steadfast and one which enters within the veil."*

Human relationships are a bit trickier. Since we have a tendency to make mistakes in our words, actions, and decisions, the past often has an association with forgiveness or lack of forgiveness. In this sense, forgiveness can be seen as God's way to clear or clean up the past. What we need is a new past, according to Romans 6:4: *Therefore we have been buried with Him through baptism into death, so that as Christ was raised from the dead through the glory of the Father, so we too might walk in newness of life.* New life comes with a new past.

Having a new past allows you to put the old away and live in the present with hope for the future. Hope based on the new Christ-given past is a spiritual thing! As a result of that hope, we don't have to let yesterday's news rob us of present and future joy in Him.

Truth

As we get to know God and others, we must understand that our knowledge is based in the truth. Jesus said this of Himself in John 14:6: *"I am the way, the truth, and the life."* Fortunately we have the Scriptures to tell us about God so that we might come to Him and accept Him as Savior, Lord, and Life. Knowing Him forms part of the long-term plan.

A vital personal relationship with the Father helps one discover His purpose, His love, His forgiveness, His grace, and the uniqueness of His creation—you! This relationship allows us to discover the riches He placed within us. It allows us to grow into unique children of God.

Human relationships can be a tricky. Knowing the complexities of our existence is a daunting task. Some have left family and friends to go "find" themselves. Here's the question: How easy is it to get to know someone who does not know themselves? What if you don't know yourself and you're trying to get to know someone who doesn't know himself, either? You get the picture—it's complex and confusing.

Fear and shame can deter individuals from knowing themselves and others. Just as Adam and Eve hid in the Garden of Eden, we hide for fear of the consequences of wrongdoing or in shame because we feel defective. To protect ourselves, we hide behind a mask designed to shroud our fear and shame. The mask presents a front or persona we want others to see. How can you experience the true you? How can you allow others to experience the true you? What is the true you?

Discovery of the true you leads you on an exciting but seemingly scary path. This is why we must know God's thoughts toward us. We need to know the truth about ourselves. This need creates our hunger to know Him in the depths of our beings. Maintaining a mask is hard work! Being human is natural. In the life of the believer revealing the Christ within is a normal process.

Trust

Trust is the belief that someone or something is reliable, good, honest, or effective. ("Will you hold my wallet while I go into the shop? I trust you, but I don't trust myself.") Trust forms an essential part of a relationship. In human relationships trust is easy to lose and difficult to find or regain. It takes time and integrity to regain trust once it's shaken.

Proverbs 3:5 tells us to trust in the Lord even when it doesn't make sense: *Trust in the Lord with all your heart and do not lean on your own understanding.* "Is it trust, or is it faith? OK, it is faith…*and* trust. We put our faith in God, and we trust Him as we face life's challenges.

Three words can sum up winters in Iowa: snow, cold, and ice. You would think someone raised in the north would trust the ice. I don't. There is a type of winter fishing called "ice fishing." No, the anglers don't fish for ice—they fish *on* ice. Watch the movie *Grumpy Old Men* if you don't know what I'm talking about. Ice fishing involves driving your vehicle out on a frozen lake while dragging a small building with a false floor. You choose a spot, cut through the ice, place the small building over the hole, and fish.

I remember the first time I walked out on an iced-over lake. I inched my way, listening for the telltale cracking sound of thin ice. I heard from off in the distance a snowmobile coming in my direction. Suddenly the snowmobile flew off the embankment and onto the lake and then sped off. In that moment I gained trust in the ice. I saw that the ice was strong enough to hold both me and a vehicle. As a result, I relaxed and enjoyed my time on the frozen lake. Walking with the Lord can be like that. Once you experience His sustaining strength through life's difficult situations, you learn to lean not on your own understanding but to put your faith and trust in His steadfastness and trustworthiness.

Trust forms an integral part of building a lasting relationship with others. In time and with truth, trust helps to establish lasting bonds.

In your relationship with God and others, ask yourself these questions:

1. Am I spending quality time with God, with my friends, and by myself?

2. Am I truthful and transparent in my relationship with God, with others, and with myself?

3. Do I trust Him to lead me? Do I trust others and give them the benefit of the doubt? Do I trust my own walk with Him?

Chapter Three

Why Do We Need Grace to Relate?

Jack and Grace have been married for twenty years. They think they should have it all figured out by now, but they still struggle in their relationship. As they sit next to each other, I can feel the tension, the pain, and the hurt. How did they get here? Where did they go wrong? Why do they just seem to tolerate each other? This doesn't seem like the godly marriage they desired so long ago. Oneness with the Lord and with others? There seems to be little oneness.

"Why are you here?" I ask the couple.

Jack responds, "Well, we need help. We love each other, but we don't like each other. And lately it's gotten to be almost unbearable."

"You don't love me!" Grace snaps.

"I told you this morning that I love you," Jack replies.

"You didn't mean it!" Grace retorts.

"Yes, I did!" Jack says defensively.

"Well, you sure don't act like it!" Grace responds.

I interject a question here. "Jack, do you feel Grace loves you?"

"I know she loves me, but I feel like I can't do anything right. It's all confusing."

"Grace, what do you honestly think and feel when Jack says he loves you?" I ask.

"I feel he just wants something or that he is just trying to smooth things over. He doesn't really mean it."

Jack and Grace have reached a crisis point in their relationship. They don't trust each other. They believe hidden agendas are at play. Each questions the other's motives and they are on the defensive at all times. It's challenging to truly love when emotional walls are so high.

Is there any hope for Jack and Grace? Yes, there is always hope, even in the most hopeless of situations. Jack and Grace need a new foundation on which to base their relationship. They need a new belief system about their new identity in Christ and how God sees His children. They need a new way of communicating. They need to forget what lies behind and allow each other and their relationship to shift into harmony. They need to forgive. It seems impossible? It is impossible without God's Grace! They need God's grace to relate.

The reason I feel compelled to write this book is summarized in its title: *Grace to Relate*. It takes grace to stay in a relationship through all the relational dead ends, cul-de-sacs, and freeways. Actually, it takes more than grace—it takes truth as well, as stated in John 1:14: *And the Word became flesh and dwelt among us, and we beheld His glory, glory as of the only begotten from the Father, full of grace and truth.*

Did you get that? Jesus is full of grace *and* truth. I have found in my many years of helping individuals that, generally, grace marries truth. What I mean is this: A person who leans toward grace tends to marry someone who leans more toward truth.

The story concerning the man with the withered hand, as recorded in Mark 3:1–6, demonstrates truth and grace: *He entered again into a synagogue; and a man was there whose hand was withered. They were watching Him to see if He would heal him on the Sabbath, so that they might accuse Him. He said to the man with the withered hand, "Get up and come forward!" And He said to them, "Is it lawful to do good or to do harm on the Sabbath, to save a life or to kill?" But they kept silent. After looking around at them with anger, grieved at their hardness of heart, He said to the man, "Stretch out your hand." And he stretched it out, and his hand was restored. The Pharisees went out and immediately began conspiring with the Herodians against Him, as to how they might destroy Him.*

Rather than compassion, the religious leaders focused on whether or not Jesus would "violate" the Sabbath by healing the man. They honed in on the letter of the law, "truth" without grace. Jesus instead focused on healing the man's condition, even though the religious leaders saw Jesus as a lawbreaker and grieved at His actions. The Pharisees' hardness of heart disappointed Jesus, but He demonstrated the truth of God's laws by acting according to the spirit of the law. He acted in grace.

The person occupied with truth sees things as black or white. He or she has a mind-set that seeks out the truth. What is the "right" thing to do? How can we order our lives in order to please God? This person's slogan could be, "Never meet in the middle. It's my way or the highway!"

Years ago a mother consulted with me, "My daughter is now a born-again believer, but over a year ago she sold drugs. What should I do now? Should I turn her in to the authorities?"

I asked the woman, "Is your daughter doing or selling drugs now?"

She responded, "No, like I said, she is born again."

This lady was struggling with the letter of the law of the state. Truth leaners can be sticklers for state law as well as God's law. She wanted to do what was right and what would please the Lord. I asked her, "What is the purpose of the law? What would be accomplished by turning your daughter in?"

The purpose of this world's drug laws is to stop people from doing or dealing drugs. The spirit of the law protects individuals from harming themselves or others. Turning the daughter in would accomplish nothing because she already had repented and turned from drugs.

So how can we balance grace and truth? The answer might surprise you: you alone cannot balance grace and truth in your life and relationships. Listen to what I am saying. You cannot will a graceful relationship into existence. Only He can provide such a relationship, through His indwelling presence in our lives. In other words, there is no magic relationship formula. If there were, you'd have little room for growth, expansion, or learning through the Lord. Make your relationship with God the most important one in your life, and watch His grace and truth pour into your union.

Rely only on Him.

Chapter Four

What Is the Basis of Our

Relationship with God?

Christ, Our Focus

Christian relationships differ from others in our culture today. The basis of these relationships makes them different. While the culturally based relationship is person-centered, the

> **Your walk with others is as deep as your walk with God**

Christian relationship is Christ-centered and empowered. Matthew 6:33 reads, *But seek first His kingdom and His righteousness, and all these things will be added to you.*

Healthy, graceful relationships form their basis in seeking Him first. Knowing Him as Savior, Lord, and Life allows us to fully plumb the depths of our relationships. It is indeed true that the depth of earthly relationships corresponds to the depth of your heavenly relationship. In other words, your walk with others is as deep as your walk with God**.** Thus, spirituality is an essential element of successful, meaningful earthly relationships.

Years ago a missionary in Africa shared a simple diagram to demonstrate the awesome effects of a God-focused life. He drew a simple triangle and at the top wrote the word "God"; on the two bottom corners, he wrote "man" on one side and "woman" on the other. As the man or woman focused and walked toward God, they naturally drew together at the pinnacle. Inside the triangle the missionary drew lines between the man and woman that got shorter and shorter as they approached the apex of God. These lines represented the petty differences that separated the man and the woman, getting smaller until they disappeared altogether at the top (see illustration).

A few years back, while I was counseling a couple, one produced "evidence" to prove how the other deliberately instigated a disagreement. That evidence consisted of two photographs, complete with date and time stamps. One photo was taken at 12:05 a.m., the other at 6:12 a.m. the same day. What was the damning evidence? Toilet paper. That's right, toilet paper. At 12:05 a.m. the paper was rolling off the top of the roll, and at 6:12 a.m. it was rolling off the bottom. The instigating spouse had switched the toilet paper during the night!

To the offended spouse this demonstrated intentional, spiteful antagonism. While this seemed critical to this couple, it is almost comical for others. Remember, though, petty things don't seem petty when they happen to you. You can only rise above the pettiness of life when you receive and know His love and grace.

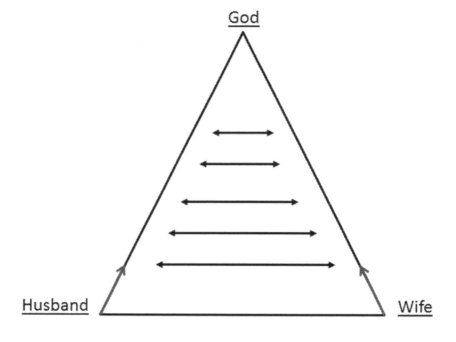

When a crisis occurs in the family, notice that as you draw nearer to the Lord, you draw nearer to each other, just like in the triangle illustration. A genuine crisis, such as a sick child or a car accident, can overshadow the true insignificance of unimportant, petty issues. In the middle of a crisis, we do not care about how the toilet paper comes off the roll. We rightfully give our attention to prayer and support of the sick or injured family member. In a crisis His grace keeps us from getting caught up in the petty and keep us focused on a person, Him.

Who Is this Christ?

As we walk with Christ, we come to know Him on different levels—as Savior, Lord, and Life.

Savior

At the first level, we know of Him and begin to consider the claims of Christ. Coming to know Christ is similar to being in a funnel. In cooking or automotive applications, a funnel guides a liquid into a bottle or can so that it does not spill. A funnel guides something from a large expanse to a small entry way. In life the sides of the funnel consist of the daily circumstances and trials we encounter. These situations make us aware of our spiritual need and lead us to explore our relationship with Him. Eventually we come to invite Christ to be our Savior because we have come to recognize our self-centeredness and need for forgiveness.

Lord

Once we move through the funnel of Christ as Savior, we move into the funnel of Christ as Lord. This new funnel is designed to bring us to a point where we realize that not only do we want Christ as our Savior but that He is Lord and desires to be so by leading and guiding us in our lives. In this funnel we realize that we are not in this funnel alone, and we try to align with His way. One friend describes Lordship as one big yes and a lot of little uh-huhs along the way. We make the big Lordship decision and reaffirm it day by day. At this stage, relating to Christ as Lord deals with the law, which creates a dilemma. If we fail or disobey Christ, we are unrighteous and feel guilty. If we do a great job in obeying Him, then we can become prideful ("Look at what a good believer I am!"). We come to realize that apart from Him we can do nothing, as illustrated in John 15:5: *"I am the vine, you are the branches; he who abides in Me and I in him, he bears much fruit, for apart from Me you can do nothing."* We realize that, apart from Him, we do not have the power to walk His way.

In Galatians 3:22 we read, *But the Scripture has shut up all men under sin, that the promise by faith in Jesus Christ might be given to those who believe.* The purpose of the Scripture is to show us that we can't obey perfectly because the Law is perfect. This inability is implied in the meaning of the phrase "*shut up all men under sin.*" We must trust Him for the righteousness He has both imputed and imparted to us through His Holy Spirit. When He says we have His righteousness then we do. We must trust what He says about us. We realize we need new life, a new source of strength to thrive.

Life

Once we understand our total inadequacy and powerlessness, we enter into a new funnel, the funnel of Christ as Life. In Colossians 3:4 Paul writes, *When Christ, who is our life, is revealed, then you also will*

> *Therefore if anyone is in Christ, he is a new creature; the old things passed away; behold, new things have come.*
> 2 Corinthians 5:17

be revealed with Him in glory. Take note of the phrase "*Christ, who is our life.*" Christ forgives us, wants to direct us, and desires to empower us through His very life within! He gives us instruction and the strength to obey—we come to know His grace. We are His children by new birth, regardless of our performance.

That last statement scares many today. Why? Some believe the only way to keep believers in line is through fear, condemnation, and guilt. They perceive a fearsome God, who judges and punishes the "imperfect." Think about this for a moment. How would you respond if your children feared you? What if your children felt you were waiting for them to step out of line so you could punish them? What if every time you approached, they cowered in the corner? I imagine you would feel grieved. Yes, the Lord does care about our performance. Performance does not determine who we are; it reveals who we are. By nature a parrot acts like a parrot, but a parrot can learn human speech. If we were asked which "animal" talks human, we would probably say a human being. Talking parrots mimic behavior but do not comprehend human speech. Parrots may use human speech, but that doesn't make them human.

DNA or AND?

There are basically two beliefs about how the Christian life works: the AND way and the DNA way.

AND

Dictionary.com defines the word "and" as, "Conjunction (grammar), a part of speech that connects two words, phrases, or clauses." In the AND way, an individual believes and sets out to be like Christ in all that they do, think, feel, and choose. I have Christ *and* I strive to do better, work harder, study more, memorize more, act more consistently, and so on. To please God, it takes believing Christ *and* performing my works.

DNA

The other belief is the DNA way. Deoxyribonucleic acid (DNA), as explained on Wikipedia.org, "is a molecule that encodes the genetic instructions used in the development and functioning of all known living organisms." In the DNA way, I possess the DNA given to me at new birth. When I

> Galatians 5:16–17 *"But I say, walk by the Spirit, and you will not carry out the desire of the flesh. For the flesh sets its desire against the Spirit, and the Spirit against the flesh; for these are in opposition to one another, so that you may not do the things that you please."*

was born again, I received my "new creature" DNA from my Father God. Now to please God, I live and develop and function as His child.

I was raised on a farm, and I like to ask people, "Do you know why pigs oink?" Pigs oink because they are pigs. Oinking doesn't *make* them pigs. Accordingly, I do His will because I am His child, not to become His child. I act like a believer because I am one, not to become one. Not only has God given us new spiritual DNA, He has given us a new heart and new spirit, as explained in Ezekiel 36:26–28: *"Moreover, I will give you a new heart and put a new spirit within you; and I will remove the heart of stone from your flesh and give you a heart of flesh. I will put My Spirit within you and cause you to walk in My statutes, and you will be careful to observe My ordinances. You will live in the land that I gave to your forefathers; so you will be My people, and I will be your God."* The most natural—and supernatural—thing I can do is walk with Him.

Some teach that we have both the old "in Adam" DNA and the new "in Christ" DNA. Pastor Andrew Farley, in his new book *Relaxing with God*, states, "If God intervenes in our lives, kills our old self, resurrects us and re-creates us for good works with a new spirit, a new heart, and God's Spirit permanently sealed within us, then what's your best guess about our spiritual nature?" DNA determines nature. Always has, always will.

Confusion comes because some have used the word "flesh" inter-changeably with the word "nature." One popular Bible translation inter-prets the Greek word *sarx* ("flesh") as nature, adding to this confusion.

Yes, the flesh is still active, but God has given each believer a new identity as His child. We are children of the King, children of royalty. What a great privilege it is to be His child, to have His life and His desires pulsing through our spirit.

Spirit-filled and Spirit-led

Another aspect of a biblical relationship involves the need for each individual to know and understand what it means to be a spirit-filled and spirit-led believer. Ephesians 5:18 states, *And do not get drunk with wine, for that is dissipation, but be filled with the Spirit.*

Spirit-filled

As believers, God commands us to fill ourselves with the Spirit. I know this is not a popular concept for some, but simply put, we cannot have a graceful Christ-centered relationship without being filled with the Holy Spirit. To be filled means to be controlled by, animated by, or empowered by the Holy Spirit. In the Ephesians 5:18 passage, "dissipation" ("debauchery" in the King James Version) speaks to the lack of focus or control (also see the Amplified version of this verse). Why is this important?

A person needs to be filled with the Spirit because only Spirit can resist the false (baited) temptations of flesh. Some believers think that if you do not carry out the desire of the flesh, then you walk in the Spirit. That is backward, in reverse. Only Spirit has the power to resist flesh. The flesh tries to restructure itself. Through fleshly manipulation and strength, the flesh is "made" to look spiritual. According to Galatians 5:16, there is no peace between the Spirit and the flesh—they will always remain at odds. Just remember that the war reflects an inward struggle of flesh versus Spirit and not an outward struggle of friend versus friend or husband versus wife. Don't forget where the real battle lies. Fortunately we know the ultimate victor: Spirit.

Spirit-led

Another aspect of the spiritual life entails being Spirit-led. Believers should walk in the Spirit. In Romans 8:14 Paul writes, *For all who are being led by the Spirit of God, these are sons of God.* Paul says that being led by the Spirit of God forms one way of knowing yourself as a child of God! Why is this

> *However, you are not in the flesh but in the Spirit, if indeed the Spirit of God dwells in you. But if anyone does not have the Spirit of Christ, he does not belong to Him.*
>
> Romans 8:9

so important? Many times in our relationships we react from our past instead of responding to God's leadership. We react out of the flesh and the old ways of handling life. It is all we know.

Besides the flesh, people can be controlled or led by their mind, will, or emotion, all steeped in old programming. For example, my natural response to conflict leads me to head for the cave to escape. My cave was my room, basically anywhere I could be alone. One day as I went on my way, the Lord gently asked, "Where are you going?"

I responded, "I'm going to my room!"

He said, "Who gave you permission to do that?"

Well, I didn't like what I sensed from Him. I didn't want to interact with the individual I felt had been rude to me just moments before. I thought he needed punishment, and I decided to exact my revenge by ignoring him, exhibiting classic passive-aggressive behavior. Fortunately I responded to Him instead of my flesh and the conflict resolved in a few short minutes as I moved into conversation with the rude individual.

I wish I could say that I always respond to His leading, but I don't. Being Spirit-led allows the Holy Spirit to lead you moment by moment. Mark 13:11 demonstrates this principle: *When they arrest you and hand you over, do not worry beforehand about what you are to say, but say whatever is given you in that hour; for it is not you who speak, but it is the Holy Spirit.*

Character Qualities

A graceful relationship also involves the God-given character qualities of a believer. What does the character of a believer look like? Galatians 5:22–23 summarizes these qualities: *The fruit of the Spirit is love, joy, peace, patience, kindness, goodness, faithfulness, gentleness, and self-control.*

These qualities dwell within the Holy Spirit. Since the believer holds the Holy Spirit within (Rom. 8:9), he or she can and should express the character qualities of the Holy Spirit. When believers say, "I don't have patience!" they are sorely mistaken. Is the Holy Spirit patient? Of course! Is the Holy Spirit loving? Of course!

Now comes that difficult question, "What do I express to others?" As brothers and sisters in Christ, or as husband and wife, we should relate according to our true character qualities: love, joy, peace, patience, kindness, goodness, faithfulness, gentleness, and self-control.

Yes, we experience lapses in character and of memory, but that does not excuse believers' responsibility for what they express to others. We deal with those lapses through confession. Confession means agreeing with God about who we are in Christ – our new identity. For example, when we feel impatience we can confess that God is patient and thank Him for giving us patience through the Holy Spirit within. We put our faith in Him to express His patience through us.

In comparison, look at Galatians 5:19–21: *The deeds of the flesh are evident, which are immorality, impurity, sensuality, idolatry, sorcery, enmities, strife, jealousy, outbursts of anger, disputes, dissensions, factions, envying, drunkenness, carousing, and things like these.*

Let me first draw your attention to the term "deeds of the flesh," and consider this question for a moment: "Is it harder to walk in the Spirit, or is it harder to walk in the ways of the flesh?" Most would immediately respond that it is much harder to walk in the Spirit! If you believe that it is harder to walk in the Spirit, I challenge you to think the question through.

These verses of Galatians 5 present two lists: "fruit of the Spirit" and "deeds of the flesh." Which sounds like work? How hard do we have to work for fruit? Perhaps the enemy has deceived us into thinking it is harder to choose righteousness over unrighteousness.

Years ago I took my two sons out to a restaurant with a breakfast buffet. Before we went through the line, I asked them to think about this question: "Is it easier to sin or to obey?" After my sons got their food, I asked for their answer and they both said they thought it was easier to sin or disobey. Choosing sin comes easily! Think about it though. If you choose to escape a situation by lying and continuing to lie, you create a habit of lying. You might even do it mindlessly, with your truth meter set on autopilot. Now, which is easier—telling the truth the first time or breaking a habit of lying? In the long haul, choosing to obey is much easier.

In summary, relate to one another according to our true qualities: love, joy, peace, patience, kindness, goodness, faithfulness, gentleness, and self-control. These qualities are gifts given to you by God and deposited in you by the Holy Spirit.

You might say, "I don't feel very loving!" But you sit in the driver's seat when it comes to steering your emotions. You can love unconditionally, or you can choose to hate. Do you prefer joy over drudgery? Most would choose the things of the Spirit if given a chance. More on that later.

Chapter Five

Why Is It So Challenging to Relate?

Some common hindrances obstruct effective and redemptive communication within relationships. Specific areas of difficulty can be found in 1 Thessalonians 5:23: *Now may the God of peace Himself sanctify you entirely; and may your spirit and soul and body be preserved complete, without blame at the coming of our Lord Jesus Christ.* In this passage we see that we have a spirit, soul and body.

The spirit of man relates to the spiritual realm, the soul of man relates to the realm of relationships with others, and the body of man allows him to relate to the physical realm.

The most common hindrances in the three areas, depicted in the diagram below, follow:

1) The body—gender differences
2) The soul—personality differences
3) The spirit—fleshly living versus spiritual living

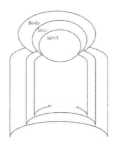

The Body—Gender Differences

Communicating with someone of the opposite sex can be quite perplexing. You see, men believe women think like men, and women believe men think like women. Of course, this is not true. It is noteworthy that many television sitcoms use these differences for comedy. In life the differences cause misunderstanding and hurt.

Some theorize that part of the reason for these misunderstandings originates in the womb. Fetuses start out pretty much undifferentiated. In the male fetus, when the Y chromosome kicks in, a number of synapses between the left and right brain are reduced. Men are truly programmed to think differently before birth! Women are born with more synapses between the left and right brain. Thus men and women tend to process information differently.

Men tend toward more "compartmentalized" thinking, while women tend toward more "global" thinking. This observation is a generalization, but many find it more often true than not. This difference has been comically demonstrated in an e-mail circulating on the Internet:

On the Differences between Men and Women

Let's say a guy named Roger is attracted to a woman named Elaine. He asks her out to a movie; she accepts, and they have a pretty good time. A few nights later he asks her out to dinner, and again they enjoy themselves. They continue to see each other regularly, and after a while both of them stop seeing anybody else.

And then, one evening when they're driving home, a thought occurs to Elaine, and without really thinking, she says it aloud: "Do you realize that, as of tonight, we've been seeing each other for exactly six months?"

And then the car fills with silence. To Elaine, it seems like a very loud silence. She thinks to herself, *I wonder if it bothers him that I said that. Maybe he's been feeling confined by our relationship. Maybe he thinks I'm trying to push him into some kind of obligation he doesn't want or isn't sure of.*

And Roger is thinking, *Wow. Six months.*

And Elaine is thinking, *But, hey, I'm not so sure I want this kind of relationship, either. Sometimes I wish I had a little more space so I'd have time to think about whether I really want us to keep going the way we are, moving steadily toward...I mean, where are we going? Are we just going to keep seeing each other at this level of intimacy? Are we heading toward marriage? Toward children? Toward a lifetime together? Am I ready for that level of commitment? Do I really even know this person?*

And Roger is thinking: *So that means it was...let's see...February when we started going out, which was right after I had the car at the dealer's, which means—lemme check the odometer...Whoa! I am way overdue for an oil change here.*

And Elaine is thinking, *He's upset. I can see it on his face. Maybe I'm reading this completely wrong. Maybe he wants more from our relationship, more intimacy, more commitment. Maybe he has sensed—even before I sensed it—that I was feeling some reservations. Yes, I bet that's it. That's why he's so reluctant to say anything about his own feelings. He's afraid of being rejected.*

And Roger is thinking, *And I'm gonna have them look at the transmission again. I don't care what those morons say; it's still not shifting right. And they'd better not try to blame it on the cold weather this time. What cold weather? It's eighty-seven degrees out, and this thing is shifting like a garbage truck, and I paid those incompetent thieves six hundred dollars.*

And Elaine is thinking, *He's angry. And I don't blame him. I'd be angry, too. I feel so guilty, putting him through this, but I can't help the way I feel. I'm just not sure.*

And Roger is thinking, *They'll probably say it's only a ninety-day warranty. That's exactly what they're gonna say, the scumballs.*

And Elaine is thinking, *Maybe I'm just too idealistic, waiting for a knight to come riding up on his white horse, when I'm sitting right next to a perfectly good person, a person I enjoy being with, a person I truly do care about, a person who seems to truly care about me. A person who is in pain because of my self-centered, schoolgirl romantic fantasy.*

And Roger is thinking, *Warranty? They want a warranty? I'll give them a stinking warranty.*

"Roger," Elaine says aloud.

"What?" says Roger, startled.

"Please don't torture yourself like this," she says, her eyes beginning to brim with tears. "Maybe I should never have—oh my, I feel so…" She breaks down, sobbing.

"What?" says Roger.

"I'm such a fool," Elaine sobs. "I mean, I know there's no knight. I really know that. It's silly. There's no knight, and there's no horse."

"There's no horse?" says Roger.

"You think I'm a fool, don't you?" Elaine says.

"No!" says Roger, glad to finally know the correct answer.

"It's just that—it's that I…I need some time," Elaine says.

There is a fifteen-second pause while Roger, thinking as fast as he can, tries to come up with a safe response. Finally he comes up with one that he thinks might work. "Yes," he says.

Elaine, deeply moved, touches his hand. "Oh, Roger, do you really feel that way?"

"What way?"

"That way about time," says Elaine.

"Oh," says Roger. "Yes."

Elaine turns to face him, causing him to become very nervous about what she might say next, especially if it involves a horse. At last she speaks. "Thank you, Roger," she says.

"Thank you," says Roger.

Then he takes her home, where she lies on her bed, a conflicted, tortured soul, weeping until dawn. Roger gets back to his place, opens a bag of Doritos, turns on the television, and immediately becomes deeply involved in a rerun of a tennis match between two Czechoslovakians he never heard of. A tiny voice in the far recesses of his mind tells him something major was going on back there in the car, but he is pretty sure there is no way he would ever understand what, and so he figures it's better if he doesn't think about it. (This is also Roger's policy regarding world hunger.)

The next day Elaine will call her closest friend, or perhaps two of them, and they will talk about this situation for six straight hours. In painstaking detail, they will analyze everything she said and every word, expression, and gesture for nuances of meaning, considering every possible ramification. They will continue to discuss this subject, off and on, for weeks, maybe months, never reaching any definite conclusions but never getting bored with it, either.

Meanwhile, Roger, while playing racquetball one day with a mutual friend of his and Elaine's, will pause just before serving, frown, and say, "Norm, did Elaine ever own a horse?"

Biblical and Cultural Differences

Just as there are differences between the way men and women think, there are also gender role differences—biblical and cultural.

While society debates, curses, or ignores the cultural differences between men and women, the Bible describes specific roles for men and women in Ephesians 5:21–33: *and be subject to one another in the fear of Christ. Wives, be subject to your own husbands, as to the Lord. For the husband is the head of the wife, as Christ also is the head of the church, He Himself being the Savior of the body. But as the church is subject to Christ, so also the wives ought to be to their husbands in everything. Husbands, love your wives, just as Christ also loved the church and gave Himself up for her, so that He might sanctify her, having cleansed her by the washing of water with the word, that He might present to Himself the church in all her glory, having no spot or wrinkle or any such thing; but that she would be holy and blameless. So husbands ought also to love their own wives as their own bodies. He who loves his own wife loves himself; for no one ever hated his own flesh, but nourishes and cherishes it, just as Christ also does the church, because we are members of His body. For this reason a man shall leave his father and mother and shall be joined to his wife, and the two shall become one flesh. This mystery is great; but I am speaking with reference to Christ and the church. Nevertheless, each individual among you also is to love his own wife even as himself, and the wife must see to it that she respects her husband.*

Some interpret these verses as teaching that women are weaker and less important than men. But 1 Peter 3:7 says, *You husbands in the same way, live with your wives in an understanding way, as with someone weaker, since she is a woman; and show her honor as a fellow heir of the grace of life, so that your prayers will not be hindered.* Husbands should live with their wives in an understanding way. Part of that understanding way means realizing just how delicate their wives are. That delicate nature could be likened to a fine china cup versus a thick, heavy coffee mug. The china cup is not inferior (weaker) when it comes to holding coffee or tea. The china cup is aesthetically pleasant and different, but that does not make it better or worse at fulfilling its purpose. Are women less important; do they have a lesser role? No, God created both men and women to glorify Him.

God expects men to provide for and protect their families, as seen in 1 Timothy 5:8: *If anyone does not provide for his own, and especially for those of his household, he has denied the faith.* As a result, one of the roles a man plays involves helping his wife and children develop their God-given gifts and abilities. An example of this principle can be found in the foreword to the book *Women as Risk-Takers for God* by Lorry Lutz and Evelyn Christenson (Baker Books 1998):

My own husband said it so well several years ago to a Japanese secular newspaper reporter in Tokyo. Mirroring his country's then male-dominated society while interviewing me about my seminar tour in their country, the obviously agitated reporter suddenly blurted, "How does your husband handle you being the teacher and speaker?" Pointing to Chris, I answered, "He's sitting right over there. Why don't you ask him for yourself?"

I listened in awe to his bold answer. "I believe the Christian husband is the spiritual head of his household, God having entrusted him with his wife and children's physical and spiritual care. The Bible says that those to whom something has been entrusted are stewards, responsible for that thing. Thus, the husband and father is the steward of the wife and children whom God has entrusted to him. That also makes him the steward of his wife's and children's gifts and talents from God. So he is responsible not only to free them to use their talents from God, He also must encourage and assist them to do so. Also, as the steward of these family members, he will give an account to God as to whether he has hindered or helped them in the use of their God-given talents."

Lastly, Ephesians 5:21 says that husbands and wives should submit to each other. Many men quote Ephesians 5:22 to remind their wives to submit, but submission goes both ways. Additionally, the Bible also tells wives to respect their husbands in Ephesians 5:33. Does that mean that men do not have to respect their wives? It is important to remember that both men and women are one in Christ, as stated in Galatians 3:28: "*There is neither male nor female; for you are all one in Christ Jesus.*" The main point I would like to make is that while gender roles might be different, men's and women's value in the kingdom is the same. Mutual love, honor, respect, and submission form the basis of a graceful marriage relationship.

"So there are the roles—now go and do these things and you will have a tremendous marriage."

* How do you respond to the above statement?
* Is the problem in troubled marriages that one does not know what to do?
* Or is the problem about not having the strength to do what one knows?

Some do not know what to do while others do not have the ability to follow through on what they have been taught. Either one can provide the answer for failing in your marital relationship. The apostle Paul uses the analogy of circumcision to teach that both the fulfillment of the law and the lack of fulfillment of the law result in a new creation in Galatians 6:15–16: *For neither is circumcision anything, nor uncircumcision, but a new creation. And those who will walk by this rule, peace and mercy be upon them, and upon the Israel of God.* This passage teaches that the essential element of becoming a new creation in Christ is vital.

Just as you can do the right thing for the wrong reasons, you can do the wrong things for the right reason. Being a new creation gives the right motive and strength, but sometimes the action is wrong. For example, "I'm going to glorify God by giving all my family's possessions to the poor." What would be wrong with that? Anything? Is there anything wrong with glorifying the Lord? Is it beyond our ability to do such a thing? The answer to all of these questions is no.

Here's the point (finally): The Lord can direct you to do things to bring Him glory, but at times we try to bring Him glory by our own direction and ability. We often intend to glorify and love God, but in our joy we try to please Him through what we think will bring glory to Him rather than through what He leads us to do.

If you want to bend your mind, read Judges 11:34 in context. No one would question Jephthah's desire to please the Lord. I'm not trying to get you to question your motives. It's God's job to reveal our motives, so says 1 Corinthians 4:5: *Do not go on passing judgment before the time, but wait until the Lord comes who will both bring to light the things hidden in the darkness and disclose the motives of men's hearts.* As we walk in our new life with Christ, we will meet our roles as husbands or wives. The question becomes: does role fulfillment result in relational fulfillment, or does relational fulfillment result in role fulfillment?

I recently heard a wife say, "My husband and I are role mates, not soul mates." When I hear such statements, I have a sense of understanding, yet that understanding is somewhat nebulous. One reason for this has to do with the concept of "soul."

Biblical psychology teaches that there are generally two beliefs concerning the makeup of man: 1) Man is two-part (dichotomous), and 2) man is three-part (trichotomous). Two-part teachers stress that man is spirit and body, with the spirit and soul being the same thing. Three-part teachers stress that the spirit, soul, and body are separate (1 Thess. 5:23).

The chart below refers to the three-part model of man. It contains four columns because the biblical roles of husband and wife do not fall into any one category. Given the woman's statement about role mates versus soul mates, there would be a difference between the oneness we have in the Spirit and the oneness we have in the soul. The soul can be defined as your personality, your mind, will, and emotions—your uniqueness as a person.

The following chart visually demonstrates the different emphasis of role in the marriage relationship. The columns define the role indicated.

The first column explains the spirit mate. The first row emphasizes the oneness, the relationship that the believing couple has with the Father. We emphasize knowing God. As soul mates, we focus on knowing each other both as a spirit mate and soul mate. This includes personality, quirks, etc.

I'm going to jump over the role mate for a minute and talk about the physical mate. The physical mate role involves getting to know the other physically through being around each other, being affectionate, or being intimate. The role mate relates to learning a role (tell me what to do and I'll do it) and keeping or performing a role (I can't do this perfectly). Practically speaking, role emphasis can be one reason why some marriage conferences do not change lives. Emphasis on the role mate aspects tends to draw the couple into a relationship based on rules and regulations (the law).

As a couple enjoys being spirit mates with the Lord, they become better soul mates and physical mates to each other and fulfill their roles (role mate).

The following rows in the chart examine various characteristics across the different role manifestations.

Spirit Mate	Soul Mate	Role Mate	Physical Mate
Oneness Know God	Oneness with spouse Know spouse	Know and keep your role Know role	"Known"—naked and not ashamed Physical Oneness
We enjoy His love and presence	Love and enjoy your spouse	Try to love and enjoy your spouse	Desire and enjoy physical closeness
Trust God	Trust or learn to trust your spouse	Trust your spouse to do their role	Trust your spouse not to physically hurt you
Oneness with God in your heart	Sense heart ties and connections with your spouse	Try to "do" oneness with spouse	Desire and feel desired for closeness and oneness
Transparency with God	Transparency with spouse	Try to be transparent with your spouse	Be transparent with your physical desires
Communication with God/ Prayer	Communication and enjoyment when talking with spouse	Try to communicate with your spouse	Communicate with attentiveness
Expression of Appreciation to God	Appreciate your spouse's uniqueness	Be thankful for your spouse's performance	Feel joy from the fulfillment of physical need
Vulnerability with God	Cautious vulnerability with your spouse	Be vulnerable with your spouse	Allow yourself to be vulnerable with your neediness

Let us now turn our attention to the area of the soul.

The Soul—Personality Differences

The soul, sometimes referred to in Scripture as the "inner man," involves that part considered to be an individual's personality. While every person has unique traits, the personality of most individuals is driven or dominated by one or more of these three elements: the mind (thinker), the will (doer), or the emotions (feeler).

An individual's personality type affects how they interpret what others say and do. Different interpretations can cause miscommunication between couples. One person interprets what the other person says or does in terms of what that person would be trying to communicate when saying or doing those things.

For example, a quiet thinker (mind) is generally thinking, but a quiet feeler (emotion) may be angry. Many times a feeler asks the thinker spouse, "What's wrong?" The question often jars the thinker back to the relationship, when he or she was simply steeped in thought, analyzing the possible source of a computer malfunction. The thinker is immediately confronted with the question of "What's wrong?" and generally doesn't have a clue. Understanding your spouse's personality can help you communicate with them in meaningful terms.

For a simple way of determining your particular personality style, highlight or check each of the following characteristics listed here. I have organized each style into regions describing basic characteristics, comfort zones, fears, relation to God, and values in the kingdom of God. This will help differentiate and contrast styles. Add up how many checks you have in each area. The area (thinker, feeler, or doer) with the highest number of checkmarks could be your primary personality motivation. Let's briefly look at common characteristics of each personality type.

THE THINKER

Basic Characteristics

- Believes tasks equal identity (how well one performs provides a sense of worth or value)
- Displays excessive mental energy (very analytical, thinking all the time)
- Tends not to be impulsive (actions are the result of having thought things through)
- Values truth and honesty; assumes and expects others to do the same
- In tasks, focuses on the 5 percent that is wrong or might go wrong rather than on the 95 percent that's good or right (seeing things as black or white)
- Has a negative self-perception—highly critical of oneself and others
- Tends to take blame
- Keeps lists religiously and feels bad if all items are not checked off
- Has a long memory when it comes to the faults of others, resulting in difficulty with forgiveness
- Can work well with others but prefers to work alone
- Recharges by being alone

Comfort Zone

- Perfectionistic doing and thinking, resulting in high standards that can be "higher" than God's ("God may forgive me, but I can't forgive myself!")
- Having thoughts and life in order
- Security in the family, the known
- Controlling or stifling of emotions
- Tendency to look to money for security

- Sense of safety in the ability to reason, know, or understand (the tendency to put trust in the ability to think something through or to understand a concept before turning to God)

Fear of...

- Antagonism in relationships (the thinker tends to "own" his or her opinions and therefore feels hurt when others disagree)
- Losing control emotionally
- Deceiving someone or being deceived
- Failure, showing imperfections

In Relationship with God

- Fears that God will not act or will make the Thinker do something insensible
- Accepts God's forgiveness but has difficulty forgiving oneself or others
- Considers failure (sin) one of the most important things although God (who has decisively already covered all sin) considers failure a means to learn all that He has provided in Christ.
- Desires to understand before believing—John 6:69: *We have believed and have come to know that You are the Holy One of God.*
- Equates God's presence with intellectual insight—John 4:24: *God is spirit; and those who worship Him must worship in spirit and truth.*

Value in the Kingdom

- Detail oriented
- Extremely loyal
- Good teacher
- Great disciple, particularly one-on-one

- Critical and analytical, which can help keep the church in check
- Rarely deviates from the teaching received

THE DOER

Basic Characteristics

- Accomplishes tasks through people, seeing their value as good workers and as tools to meet a goal
- Displays excessive volitional energy (strong-willed)
- Acts to meet goals, or to get a thrill (jumping out of airplanes)
- Finds value in accomplishing goals
- Focuses on the objective or goal and cannot see obstacles
- Determines self-perception by successes and accomplishments
- Tends to give blame ("If others had just…then things would have worked out")
- Uses lists to increase productivity
- Likes to be in charge of the work group
- Recharges through taking a challenge or risk

Comfort Zone

- Being in control, without restrictions on time or resources
- Security in others (seeing them as important, significant, and influential)
- Embracing change and moving toward a goal
- Avoiding feelings (no utility in emotions—except anger)
- Feeling of safety in one's abilities and willpower

Fear of…

- Boredom in life and relationships
- Giving control to others

- Being insignificant by failing to accomplish tasks and goals
- Routine

In Relationship with God

- Seeks God under extreme pressure
- Desires to see the power of God
- Equates the work of God with His personal presence
- Respects the power of God but with some trepidation—*Let Him now come down from the cross, and we shall believe in Him* (Matt. 27:42)

Value to the Kingdom

- Initiates change
- Motivates others to accomplish goals, in spite of obstacles
- Not sidetracked by others' complaints
- Can stand up under the most vicious attacks
- Defender of the faith

THE FEELER

Basic Characteristics

- Bases identity on relationships (relationship success or failure)
- Displays excessive emotional energy and feels things deeply
- Is motivated by fun
- Values relationships and quality time with people
- Has a hard time staying on task, especially when people are present
- Determines self-perception based on others' acceptance
- Tends to take blame ("People would accept me if I did everything right!")
- Loses lists religiously

- Has a short memory when it comes to the faults of others
- Finds forgiveness in allowing others to fail
- Likes to "work" in a group
- Recharges by being with people

Comfort Zone

- Being accepted and liked in relationships; being sought after by others
- Having relationships in order
- Seeking change and variety in activities
- Pleasant emotions (avoids negative feelings)
- Feeling confident in the ability to keep everyone happy

Fear of...

- Complex or difficult relationships (seeks agreement through persuasion)
- A controlled environment that doesn't allow for expression or impulsiveness
- Harming or being harmed by others
- Failure in relationships, rejection from others

In Relationship with God

- Constantly feels rejected when unable to feel God's presence or verbally hear His affirmations
- Must learn to live out of the fact, not the feeling, of who God is; meditating on who God is, who he is in Christ, and what God says
- Needs time alone with God to bask in the truth, because a Feeler tends to confuse facts and feelings
- Needs variety in the walk with God

- Must see the possibility of having a deep relationship with God without the feelings. Must be secure in His acceptance in order to not rely too heavily on others acceptance—*How can you believe when you receive glory from one another and you do not seek the glory that is from the one and only God* (John 5:44)?
- Fights impulse to run from God in the face of a perceived failure
- Wants to feel or experience God before believing instead of the other way around ("If you let me experience You then I'll believe!")—*He who hears My word, and believes Him who sent Me, has eternal life* (John 5:24).
- Equates God's presence with feelings: *God is spirit, and those who worship Him must worship in spirit and truth* (John 4:24).

Value to the Kingdom

- Tuned in to hurts, needs, and feelings of others, often offering empathy and compassion
- Sees good in others and desires to give second chances
- Ability to encourage and enjoy that role
- Leading through persuasion, believing things always get better

Now that we've looked at the body and soul, let's turn our attention to the Spirit.

The Spirit—Fleshly Living versus Spiritual Living

No one can quite frustrate you like your spouse or someone very close to you. It almost seems the closer you get to someone, the harder it becomes to relate in times of trouble. In most relationships we eventually need grace to relate.

Why is it so challenging to relate with someone close to you? I am taking the truth of Galatians 5:17, *For the flesh sets its desire against the*

Spirit, and the Spirit against the flesh; for these are in opposition to one another, and demonstrating how both spouses' flesh-based choices cause misery and misunderstanding within the relationship, even if one spouse is walking in the Spirit and the other in the flesh.

What is this flesh that causes so much trouble? The term "flesh" refers to that part of the believer that chooses to live by its own earthly direction and resources instead of the Lord's. While the soul part of man (mind, will, and emotion) can influence the flesh, flesh and personality are not synonymous.

Before finding Christ, an individual lives from his or her soul because the spirit is dead to God. The lessons learned while attempting to navigate life without God are commonly referred to as "flesh." Flesh is unwilling and unable to submit itself to God; it rebels against God. Romans 8:6: *For the mind set on the flesh is death, but the mind set on the Spirit is life and peace.*

Dealing Biblically with the Flesh

The first thing that must be done, which already has been gained in Christ, is that we live as though we are dead to the flesh. We can do this because we *are* dead to the flesh. The following verses demonstrate this:

Jesus answered them, saying, "The hour has come for the Son of Man to be glorified. Truly, truly, I say to you, unless a grain of wheat falls into the earth and dies, it remains alone; but if it dies, it bears much fruit. He who loves his life loses it, and he who hates his life in this world will keep it to life eternal" (John 12:23, 25).

That which you sow does not come to life unless it dies (1 Cor. 15:36).

Bearing fruit requires the death of the seed in order for life to result. This is often called the death/life cycle, which we will examine in the next chapter. In summary we should be dead, or nonresponsive, to the flesh but then walk, led by and responsive to the Spirit. Galatians 5:16 expresses this truth: *Walk by the Spirit, and you will not carry out the desire of the flesh.* Let's examine the death part of the death/life cycle.

The Stronghold of the Flesh Has Been Broken

The seed (grain of wheat) has a shell that contains an embryo (see the next illustration). The shell prevents nourishment from occurring before the seed is planted. The shell also protects the embryo and holds it in stasis until the proper time. The seed must first enter into the darkness (in the soil). Three conditions must be met in order for the outer shell to be cracked, allowing the seed to grow: 1) temperature (light), 2) moisture, and 3) oxygen. In spiritual growth, could it be that in order for His life (embryo) within to be revealed it must first break out of the shell (the flesh)? Could it be that the flesh must come to the end of its false life pursuits and self-protective ways in order to grow in Christ? Once the conditions are met (temperature, oxygen, and water), the life within breaks free of the shell (still in darkness) and grows toward the warm, life-giving sun. As long as the shell remains intact, it hinders nourishment from our Lord. Read the following verses to see His provision for this process…

Light

*In Him was life, and the life was the **Light** of men* (John 1:4).

*Jesus again spoke to them, saying, "I am the **Light** of the world; he who follows Me will not walk in the darkness, but will have the **Light** of life"* (John 8:12).

*For God, who said, "**Light** shall shine out of darkness," is the One who has shown in our hearts to give the **Light** of the knowledge of the glory of God in the face of Christ* (2 Cor. 4:6).

Water

*He who believes in Me, as the Scripture said, "From his innermost being will flow rivers of living **water**"* (John 7:38).

> *You visit the earth and cause it to overflow;*
> *You greatly enrich it;*
> *The stream of God is full of **water**;*
> *You prepare their grain, for thus You prepare the earth.*
> *You **water** its furrows abundantly,*
> *You settle its ridges,*
> *You soften it with showers,*
> *You bless its growth* (Ps. 65:9–10).

> *He will be like a tree firmly planted by streams of **water**,*
> *Which yields its fruit in its season*
> *And its leaf does not wither;*
> *And in whatever he does, he prospers* (Ps. 1:3).

Breath

Then the LORD God formed man of dust from the ground, and breathed into his nostrils the breath of life; and man became a living being (Gen. 2:7).

The process of brokenness requires the destruction of our fleshly, fruitless, fickle, frustrating attempts to meet our needs without God. We need to come to a place where we give up on our fleshly methods to protect and nourish our souls. The protective shell must be buried and cracked, *resulting in growth and fruit.*

Remember that the shell develops as a way to protect the individual from rejection, pain, and hurt. The shell represents the response to hurt and pain: an attempt to protect oneself from future hurt or pain.

Not all protection is wrong. Children need protection and nourishment. Good protection allows good things in and keeps bad things out. In this sense protection can be good spiritually.

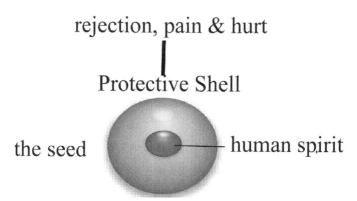

rejection, pain & hurt

Protective Shell

the seed   human spirit

What are some the fleshly ways that we must break to release His life within? While some of our patterns of thoughts and behaviors arise from an attempt to protect ourselves, they can become too rigid and hinder growth.

Ways people try to prevent pain

Quietness, withdrawal, passiveness: Some use these to "protect" themselves and their spouses. ("If you really knew me, you'd reject me. If you reject me, you really don't reject me because you don't really know me.") In a sense we hide from our spouses. These protective behaviors can be fear-based and anger-based at the same time. Such anger-based behaviors are called passive-aggressive behavior. ("I'm going to punish you by withholding myself spiritually, emotionally, or physically.")

False beliefs about your spouse's motives: An example of one possible false belief is, "You don't love and accept me." This person goes into a situation believing he or she has already been rejected in order to avoid disappointment when it happens. Another belief could be, "My spouse just wants to control me." Every word or action looks like an attempt to control.

Anger, tantrums, attacks, and meanness: These flesh patterns are overly aggressive ways to keep people at arm's length or to get them to "back off." Would you want to snuggle up to your spouse if he acted this way? These fear-inducing methods allow the person to control and manipulate others. Insecurity creates the basis for these methods. The more insecure the person, the greater his or her reaction to perceived threat. In this sense the "strong" person can be in actuality the most insecure.

Superiority, opinionatedness, judgmentality: People of this type assume they know more, deserve more, and stand above their spouses. These people consider their spouses inferior, stupid, and low-statured, so they discount or diminish messages their messages.

Defensiveness: Think about the whole seed concept. When you become defensive, what are you really trying to protect? Believers basically have two identities: 1) spiritual identity, our new identity in Christ, and 2) fleshly identity, who we feel we are when following the flesh. Why would you try to defend your identity in Christ? You don't. You want your new identity in Christ exposed to the world so you can be as in Philippians 2:15: *So that you will prove yourselves to be blameless and innocent, children of God above reproach in the midst of a crooked and perverse generation, among whom you appear as lights in the world.* So what are you defending? Your flesh-based identity? You would protect that identity only when trying to keep the flesh from exposure to the light. God sets His desire against the flesh (Gal. 5:17), asking us not to protect, reform, or rehabilitate the flesh. Defensiveness reveals our reluctance to crucify the flesh with its passions and desires.

Pretending: Have you heard the saying, "Put on your game face"? The phrase can imply that you have no game. So you pretend that you are strong, but under the mask you are weak. It can be said that the deeper the pain, the greater the pretending. Do you pretend everything is OK? Do you just try to fulfill your role as a spouse while sensing no real relational intimacy? Is there a difference between pretending and walking by faith? I believe that there is a difference. Walking by faith is truth based. The faith walk involves believing what God says about yourself or others and acting on that truth. Pretending involves acting like something is true when you really believe or feel otherwise. Pretending only works for a while before it becomes self-deception.

Distrust: What happens when you trust your spouse and he or she ends up doing something that you find hurtful or betraying? What happens when you feel deceived? You begin to view your spouse as untrustworthy. Malice means simply attributing evil to what a person says and does regardless of the circumstance. Malice is a form of distrust because you distrust your spouse's motives.

Vagueness: You can be vague when communicating your wants and desires in order to keep your spouse "on his toes" in trying to meet your needs and make you happy. Your spouse tries to get it right but can never do enough. ("If you would just do the 'right' combination of things, then I would let you in.") Vague people make their spouses prove themselves over and over with the promise, "I will trust you again." Ask the vague spouse when enough is enough, and he or she often says, "I'll know it when I see it!"

How Do We Seek to Nourish Flesh without God?

What do you seek in order to find life? What makes you feel alive? Where do you go for a sense of self-importance, purpose, and meaning? Basically, what does the flesh seek for nourishment? Here are a few things many seek:

Human respect and value: "I need you to respect and value me. In fact, I *demand* that you respect and value me. I must feel respected and valued in order to have meaning in my life."

Human love: "You must love me or I am nothing." Is feeling loved the same as being loved? Love demanded never satisfies.

Adrenaline or pleasure: "I want to feel alive, so I do extreme skiing, cutting, skydiving, or anything dangerous. I need excitement like football, television, movies, pornography, etc. Adrenaline is very, very addictive. Eating reminds me I am alive. Sex reminds me that I am loved and someone wants me." All forms of pleasure seek to counteract pain and hurt while seeking affirmation of life, love, or significance.

Elements of Victory Over the Flesh

But I say, walk by the Spirit, and you will not carry out the desire of the flesh. For the flesh sets its desire against the Spirit, and the Spirit against the flesh; for these are in opposition to one another, so that you may not do the things that you please (Gal. 5:16–17).

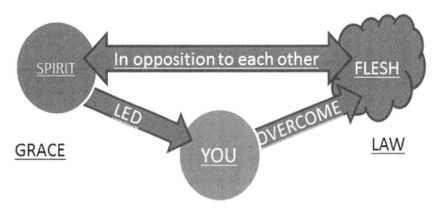

The first sentence of this passage reveals the solution to overcoming the flesh—*walk by the Spirit*. If you walk by the Spirit, you will not carry out the desire of the flesh; it doesn't say that you won't be tempted by the flesh. As we see from Galatians 5:16–17, the flesh sets its desire against the Spirit as the Spirit sets its desire against the flesh. There's a battle going on within. No surprise there! But what if you didn't realize there is a difference between you and the flesh?

In the passage above, did you notice "you" mentioned three times? As a believer you have the Spirit of God and you have access to God, but you are not God. Similarly you have the flesh and you have access to the flesh, but you are not the flesh. Just as we have a new identity in Christ, we have a fleshly identity. My true identity as a believer means being a "Christ one" or God's child. Paul refers to the believer as a new creation in 2 Corinthians 5:17. As a new creation I am a child of God. This new creation is who I am in the truest sense. If you don't differentiate between being a new creation and being fleshly then you battle (war) with God.

If you consider yourself a failure, unloved, or worthless, that is the fleshly identity—it's not you. The truth about you in Christ is revealed in 2 Corinthians 5:17: *Therefore if anyone is in Christ, he is a new creature; the old things passed away; behold, new things have come.* So what happens when you listen to the temptations of the flesh?

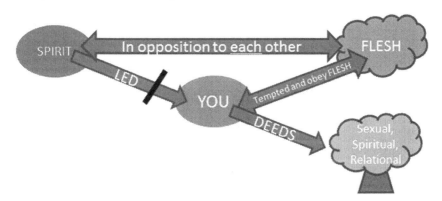

Each one is tempted when he is carried away and enticed by his own lust. Then when lust has conceived, it gives birth to sin; and when sin is accomplished, it brings forth death. Do not be deceived, my beloved brethren (James 1:14–16).

The flesh tempted and enticed you. The basic belief behind temptation is that for you to be happy, feel alive, or fulfilled, you need whatever tempts you in order to gain life or feel alive. This temptation creates a lure, a bait that promises life and delivers death. A fishing lure does the same thing. When you take the bait, the promised fulfillment turns to guilt and shame. James 1:15 explains it this way: *When lust has conceived, it gives birth to sin; and when sin is accomplished, it brings forth death.* When we yield to the temptation of the flesh, we see the deeds of the flesh…

The Deeds of the Flesh

Now the deeds of the flesh are evident, which are: immorality, impurity, sensuality, idolatry, sorcery, enmities, strife, jealousy, outbursts of anger, disputes, dissensions, factions, envying, drunkenness, carousing, and things like these, of which I forewarn you, just as I have forewarned you, that those who practice such things shall not inherit the kingdom of God (Gal. 5:19–21).

The list of the deeds of the flesh could be classified into at least four headings:

Sexual Sins

Immorality: The Greek word *porneia* can be translated "fornication." Immorality has a strong association with harlotry. The root word means "to sell," and as such refers to prostitutes and prostitution.

Immorality includes the following:

- Adultery, which refers to sexual relations with someone other than one's spouse, or an unmarried person having sexual relations
- Harlotry and prostitution and other forms of sexual sin, such as homosexuality and bestiality (see Rev. 2:14, 20)
- Note: See Matt. 5:32, 19:9; 1 Cor. 7:2; 1 Thess. 4:3 for other forms of immorality.

Impurity: The Greek word *akatharsia* means "filthiness" or "uncleanness," including not only the act of sex but also the evil thoughts and intentions of the mind.

Sensuality: The Greek word *aselgeia* refers to a lack of restraint resulting in sexual excess. *They, having become callous, have given themselves over to sensuality, for the practice of every kind of impurity with greediness* (Eph. 4:19).

Spiritual Sins

Idolatry: The Greek word *eido lolatreia* refers to taking God out of the picture and becoming your own god. Idolatry means allowing anything to become more important than God. Whatever is of self-effort without God's provision is a work of the flesh. Idolatry often manifests in a dependence on illicit drugs and in various compulsive behaviors; even our emotions can become an idol.

Sorcery: The Greek word *pharmakeia* has to do with the use of drugs and potions in ungodly rituals designed to deceive and control. It is the basis of the English word "pharmacy," but it does not forbid moderate or occasional use of medication.

Relational Sins

Enmities: The Greek word *echthra* means "hostility," an inner motivation that attempts to justify our treatment of others, the outward expression. Only God's love can replace an attitude of hatred.

Strife: The Greek word *eris* means "strife." Mostly, believers quarrel over minor issues that distract from the major things of life, like loving one another (see Matt. 22:36–40).

Jealousy: The Greek word *zelos* refers to "someone who wants what other people have." Jealousy involves lacking gratitude to the Lord for the talents and abilities He's given you, instead coveting someone else's assets.

Anger outbursts: The Greek word *thumos* means a sudden flash of anger, not a continuous state of anger. It refers to the inability to control one's temper.

Disputes: The Greek word *eritheia* describes the kind of work done for money only. It also describes selfish ambition with little conception of service, with attitudes and actions that fulfill profit and power. It is like Ray in the movie *Field of Dreams*, who asks, "What's in it for me?"

Dissensions: The Greek word *dichostasia* refers to a "standing apart," or sense of division or disconnection. It means a dissension similar to that of the Pharisees, who could not stand being around those "evil doers."

Factions: The Greek word *hairesis* describes a person or group who divisively express their choices or opinions. It means mainly the wrongful division over opposing opinions.

Envy: The Greek word *phthonos* is about being bitter because someone else has something you don't. It differs from envy in that it involves the feeling that God is playing favorites.

Self-Governance Sins

Drunkenness: The Greek word *methe* is highlighted in Ephesians 5:18: *Do not get **drunk** with wine, for that is **dissipation**, but be filled with the Spirit.* Here Paul describes drunkenness as dissipation or "wastefulness."

Carousing: The Greek word *komos* refers to *unrestrained* partying. William Barclay writes, "It means unrestrained revelry, enjoyment that has degenerated into license" (<u>The Letters to the Galatians and Ephesians</u> Revised Edition, Westminster Press, 1976, page 49).

The above list is not exhaustive and can include other things:

- Self-righteousness
- Boastful pride of life
- Judgmental ways
- Self-centeredness
- Confidence in yourself alone
- Seeking sufficiency without any outside help
- Arrogance
- And other similar traits

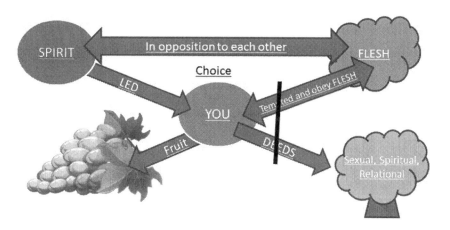

But the fruit of the Spirit is love, joy, peace, patience, kindness, goodness, faithfulness, gentleness, self-control; against such things there is no law (Gal. 5:22–23).

As we are led by the Spirit, believing and trusting in His provision, we reap the results of the fruit of the Spirit: love, joy, peace, patience, kindness, goodness, faithfulness, gentleness, and self-control. The fruit of the Spirit describes some characteristics of the Holy Spirit as well as God the Father and Jesus Christ.

Have you been walking in the freedom Christ purchased for you? Are you experiencing the victorious Christian life?

But thanks be to God, who gives us the victory through our Lord Jesus Christ (1 Cor. 15:57).

Victory over the flesh is key to enjoying a graceful marriage. We receive victory through Jesus Christ as we abide in Him. Victory is not a goal we achieve but a lifestyle we experience because it has been purchased and provided through the Lord Jesus.

Chapter Six

The Flesh Cycle

1 Samuel 18

To help you understand the flesh and its development within the believer, I want to walk you through an incident in the life of an Old Testament character named Saul. Saul seems to personify someone living in the ways of the flesh. Granted, Saul had his good days, but we have come to see him as an example of how to walk in the flesh and not according to the Spirit. Please don't misunderstand. Saul isn't perfect flesh personified, just as David isn't the perfect spiritual man, yet David was a man after God's own heart.

What was Saul's role in Israel toward the end of his rule? Saul had rejected God, and God had rejected Saul as king (see 1 Sam. 15). Saul was not spiritually minded but controlled by his flesh. What was happening in David and Saul's relationship? Here's the context:

1. David came to visit the battlefield to bring his brothers supplies. He was too young to join the army. Goliath challenged him and David killed Goliath (1 Sam. 17).

2. Saul's son Jonathan and David had formed a friendship and commitment to each other (1 Sam. 18:1–4).

3. Whatever David sought to do was blessed with success. David prospered in whatever Saul sent him out to do (1 Sam. 18:5).

4. David was esteemed in the eyes of the people and Saul's servants (1 Sam. 18:5).

5. David was publicly praised for destroying Israel's enemies by the tens of thousands, while Saul was attributed with only thousands killed. Saul became envious and looked on David with suspicion from that day on (1 Sam. 18:6–9).

How would a fleshly individual, a king, react to such attention being given to a subordinate? The following lists how Saul responded:

1. Saul looked on David with suspicion (1 Sam. 18:9).

2. Saul tried to kill David with a spear (1 Sam. 18:11).

3. Saul was afraid of David (1 Sam. 18:12). Why? The Spirit was with David and not Saul. What did Saul fear? Saul feared losing his kingdom and popularity (1 Sam. 18:8). Saul equated popularity with kingship. He needed man's approval more than God's.

4. Saul couldn't be around David (1 Sam. 18:13).

5. Saul dreaded David (1 Sam. 18:15).

6. Saul tried to deceive David through his daughters (1 Sam. 18:17).

7. He wanted the Philistines to kill David (1 Sam. 18:25).

8. He tried to control David through Michal (I Sam. 18:21).

9. Saul commanded Jonathan and his servants to kill David (1 Sam. 19:1).

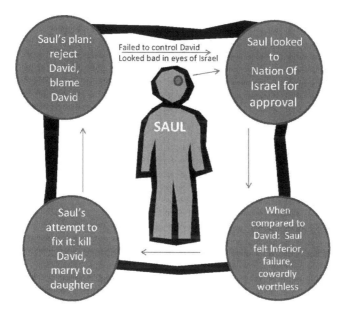

What does the flesh cycle look like in Saul's life? Saul looked to the nation of Israel for his identity, his worth and value. He received life identity messages such as, "I'm inferior to David."

Saul disliked that message. He wanted to be the center of attention, so he set out to do something about it. Saul tried to get rid of David by attempting to kill him. Frustrated by his lack of success, Saul became angry. In his anger he blamed David for the way he felt. Anger toward someone always results in some sort of separation—physical, emotional, or both.

Saul occasionally came to his senses, realizing he was wrong. Then he had more of a problem. How could the nation of Israel respect him when he had been so mean to the most popular hero? This problem reinforced his life's identity messages and around the cycle he went.

Saul continued to become more and more obsessed with getting rid of David. Just think about it for a moment. Did Saul really have anything to fear from David? What would have happened if Saul had accepted David and allowed David to lead the army? Perhaps Saul could have become one of the greatest kings of Israel. He definitely wouldn't have led such a tormented life!

Apply this cycle to our life: How did our focus on flesh develop?

The Mirror Tells Us Who We Are

As children, we look to other people to determine who we are. We look into others' faces to learn something about ourselves. Consider for a moment what you would know about yourself if somehow you were born on a deserted island and grew up without ever interacting with another human being. You would compare yourself to palm trees, monkeys, and other objects on the island in order to determine your identity. In this sense, we develop another's image rather than a self-image.

Generally we determine our self-image in large part from others' perceptions of us. Back to the mirror. The main problem with the people mirror is that the message becomes distorted because people are imperfect. This is not to blame those people but just to establish the fact that we tend to get our distorted self-image from others.

Imagine going to the hall of mirrors at the circus and believing every image we saw showed how we really looked! How confused would we be? Scripture demonstrates this principle in 2 Corinthians 3:18: *But we all, with unveiled face, beholding as in a mirror the glory of the Lord, are being transformed into the same image from glory to glory, just as from the Lord, the Spirit.*

As we behold the glory of the Lord, we are transformed into His image. This transformation emphasizes the importance of reading His word daily. In principle, what we give attention to, or focus on, transforms us. So as children, as we focus on our parents and others, we are transformed. Because people are imperfect, this transformation can be distorted. Knowing what we are and what we look like as a child of God helps give us a proper perspective of ourselves regardless of what we may see at the moment.

Life Messages Received

The individual receives life messages as he or she looks into the mirror of imperfect people. Suppose Dad is an alcoholic. What kinds of confusing life messages could a child receive?

One day the child comes home from school, and Dad is drunk, demanding, and mean. The child may wonder what he's done to cause such a response. Possible life messages might include these: "Maybe Dad just doesn't like me!" or "I'm really causing him misery," or "I'm a bad person!"

The next day the child comes home from school, and dad is sober and feeling guilty about the way he behaved the day before, so he buys things for the child to try to compensate for his cruelty. Talk about confusing the child! The child doesn't know what to expect from one day to the next. There is no connection between the child's behavior and the father's treatment. What are some typical life messages received from relating to imperfect people?

Life's Identity Messages

The list on the next page gives the possible negative feelings, or negative life identity messages, we could receive as we look into the mirror.

How can we discover our own life identity messages? You can find the answer to that question by asking yourself *this* question: "How do I see myself at my worst?" Examining how you feel about yourself at your worst often reveals the life identity messages that form the basis of your fleshly identity.

Why examine these negative emotions? Emotions exist for a reason. They help us realize what we are thinking, because behind every emotion lies a thought. For example, I feel shy in a group because I believe I don't fit in with that crowd. I'm different, and I don't know anyone.

By examining my feeling of shyness, I determine my thoughts and beliefs. Examining my emotions helps me realize I think of myself as a misfit, someone others probably wouldn't want to get to know. Therefore, I feel and act shy.

A group of thoughts form my "belief system." Feelings are useful tools that can lead to the belief system behind the feelings. Feelings help us determine what we falsely believe about ourselves at our worst. This belief system can also be referred to as our fleshly identity.

When negative thoughts surface, we can examine whether or not they are lying to us. It is important to realize we do lie to ourselves. Think about it. You're sitting in a movie theater watching a movie, and the killer quietly appears behind the "good" guy. What are you feeling? Fear, right? But you are perfectly safe. What are you afraid of? You see, you've gotten caught up in the "reality" of a fictional story.

Only when you reevaluate the truth of your emotions and believe that truth can you begin to heal. On the following short list of identity-based feelings, check off those you have experienced when at your worst:

- Abused
- Boring
- Can't do anything right
- Disrespected
- Failure
- Guilty
- Helpless
- Insignificant

- Incapable
- Suicidal
- Miserable
- Neglected
- Not good enough
- Damaged
- Stupid
- Unacceptable
- Unwanted
- Unlovable
- Worthless
- Fill in the blank

If we felt all of those feelings at one time, life would certainly be difficult! Needless to say, such feelings cause discomfort. How do we deal with these uncomfortable feelings?

How Can I Undo or Fix How I Feel?

We tend to try to undo or to fix our perceived or felt deficiencies whether or not they are true. We either try to invalidate the source of the negative identity messages or we try to fix ourselves because we have come to the conclusion that "I need to change!"

We falsely believe that if we can change enough, we will feel better about ourselves. In and of ourselves, we do not have the ability to truly change. This is a hard statement. Most people believe they can make the necessary changes. A verse that always intrigues me is John 15:5: *I am the vine, you are the branches; he who abides in Me and I in him, he bears much fruit, for apart from Me you can do nothing.*

Jesus makes it fairly clear that without Him not much can be done. Sadly, I spent many years trying to prove Jesus's words to be false. It resulted in much pain and anguish. In Acts 17:28, Paul makes reference to just how much we truly need the Lord as he explains God to the Greeks: *For in Him we live and move and exist, as even some of your own poets have said, "For we also are His children."*

The other way people try to eliminate those feelings involves invalidating those who gave them the messages. Suppose I went to visit a fellow in a mental institution and said to him, "Hi, my name is Scott," and he responded "No you're not—you're a rabbit." I would probably smile, pat him on the shoulder, and continue talking to him. Why? I evaluated the source of the comment—a mentally unstable individual—so the comment didn't bother me. Now, suppose I went home and my wife looked at me and said, "You're a rabbit!" I would probably respond differently to her.

The following lists common things individuals do to try to change the way they feel about themselves. How have you attempted to fix yourself or your circumstances? Check the ones that you've used:

- Bible study
- Counseling
- Church attendance
- Exercise
- New job
- New location
- New relationships
- Distraction in childrearing
- People pleasing
- Performance
- Prayer used as a cosmic slot machine
- Reading books
- Working harder
- Vows

Eventually these methods will fail due to various reasons.

1. Imperfect People. Some of the above mechanisms depend on the responses of imperfect people. What kind of people do we try to please in order to feel loved and accepted? Imperfect people. What kind of people do we try to develop new relationships with? Imperfect people. What kind of people do we perform for? Imperfect people. What are the chances of getting perfect love and acceptance from imperfect people? Zero.

2. Information versus Relationship. Another reason these mechanisms fail is that we use information to try to fix relational problems. The negative messages based on fleshly identity and the resulting feelings are the product of imperfect relationships. How relational is a book? What are the chances of getting perfect love and acceptance from a book? Zero. Information might help an individual see the relational nature of the problem, but information itself is nonrelational. The negative messages based on fleshly identity can only be undone in a relationship with a perfect person.

Who is the only perfect person in the world? Jesus. This is why a day-by-day relationship with Jesus creates the only solution to this "false" identity syndrome. Thefreedictionary.com defines a syndrome as "a group of symptoms that collectively indicate or characterize a disease, a psychological disorder, or another abnormal condition. A complex of symptoms indicating the existence of an undesirable condition or quality. A distinctive or characteristic pattern of behavior."

The false identity syndrome, then, is the collective results or effects of living under an identity thought to be true that is *not* true. The syndrome forms from beliefs, thoughts, feelings, and actions that, while confirmed by personal history, are known to be untrue by nature.

A pig can be trained to act like a dog, but birth dictates a pig is a pig. New birth gives the believer a renewed identity, an identity that can take months and years to fully realize. If a pig could exchange his pig's nature for a dog's nature, then training him to act like a dog would mean training him to reveal the truth—that he is indeed a dog. How many believers feel that acting holy through obedience actually makes them holy?

When we fail to fix our identity messages through the mechanisms mentioned above, we naturally respond with anger. Anger can result from a blocked goal. Suppose it's a hot day and you are very thirsty. You put three quarters in a pop machine and don't get a can of pop. How would you feel? Your goal was a cool fresh drink, and a faulty machine blocked that goal. The result? Anger.

When we look to others for love and acceptance, and then don't get that love and acceptance, we can feel angry. How do people commonly demonstrate anger? Simply put, some explode, others implode, and many do both.

The following list demonstrates mechanisms people use to try to avoid painful reminders of those negative life messages. Mark the ones that describe things you've done at your worst or lowest:

- Alcohol use
- Attention getting
- Blame
- Control
- Cheating
- Criticism of self
- Criticism of others
- Crying
- Drug use
- Exploding
- Fantasy
- Gambling
- Lying
- Manipulation
- Making excuses

- Moodiness
- Reading for escape
- Rejection of others
- Romance seeking
- Running away
- Sexual deviance
- Compulsive spending
- Stealing
- Lack of accountability
- Accepting all blame
- Excessive television
- Becoming withdrawn
- Worry
- Workaholism

Why or how do we use these mechanisms? Many try to avoid or fix, apart from God, what they perceive to be wrong. When this attempt fails, some withdraw from people. I call this withdrawing to "the cave." When the individual retreats into the cave, he doesn't have to worry about receiving those negative life messages from the people in his life.

The Fleshly Identity Addiction Cycle

People withdraw in order to be alone or protected from hurt by others. Mirrors are useless in a dark cave. The mirror of imperfect sinful people becomes null and void as we retreat into our caves. When others notice we've withdrawn into our caves, they can grab their flashlights and come into the cave to find us. Since we want to be alone, we get angry with the intruder. We demonstrate this anger by exhibiting moodiness, exploding, becoming critical of others, and performing other actions to either drive others out of our cave or to try to control how they relate to us. We act in ways that will allow us to avoid those fleshly life messages.

Let's suppose that you are successful at getting others to leave you alone or to treat you in such a way that you don't feel those negative life messages. Who do you find in the cave? You find yourself. Who do you suppose you begin to focus on? Yourself. You become critical of yourself. You see all the wrong you have done. You begin to take all the blame for the problems of life. You worry about the future and regret past actions. Then you focus on others and their role in your problems. You can start to make excuses and blame others for your problems. Eventually you see the futility of all this introspection.

How much introspection is enough? For some people it's just a little more! You come to a place where you see that you need a break from yourself. How do you escape when all else fails? One way involves escaping into someone else's world. How do you do that? You escape through books, television, music, computers, etc. You can also escape through drugs, alcohol, and sex. You may use all of these things to try to avoid all those fleshly identity messages or to undo those messages. Some of the escape methods often become addictions. You become trapped by the things you use to escape life.

Now something interesting happens. You look into the mirror and see yourself and all your bad feelings, failures, and disobedience. As you look into the mirror and see yourself, what does it tell you? It tells you that you are a failure, worthless, unacceptable, etc. The mirror confirms your worst fears. You really are what you've tried to avoid becoming or feeling. Now follow me through the process one more time. If you confirm the messages, you try to change; you fail, you get angry, you try to avoid or cope, and you confirm your messages. We find ourselves in the same place that the Apostle Paul found himself in Romans 7:24, which reads, "*Wretched man that I am! Who will set me free from the body of this death?*" Eventually, going round and round this identity addiction cycle results in depression, hopelessness, helplessness, self-condemnation, self-hatred, self-loathing, and, finally, suicidal thoughts. While we may have various addictions like overeating, alcohol, and drugs, if we fix these addictions without dealing with the fleshly identity addiction, what have we really accomplished? What is the solution for a fleshly identity addiction? We need a new identity. Where can we find a new identity? We can find a new identity in Christ.

Chapter Seven

New Identity in Christ

Paul summarizes the solution in Romans 7:25: *Thanks be to God through Jesus Christ our Lord!* Only as we understand that the former man has been crucified with Christ (Gal. 2:20), that we have been given new life in Christ (Col. 3:4), and that we therefore possess a new identity based on His life and not ours, will we begin to live with a new identity.

A battle wages between our fleshly identity and our spiritual identity. My negatively fleshly identity is at odds with my new identity in Christ. In 2 Peter 1:2–4 we see that in Christ God has already provided all that we need: *Grace and peace be multiplied to you in the knowledge of God and of Jesus our Lord; seeing that His divine power has granted to us everything pertaining to life and godliness, through the true knowledge of Him who called us by His own glory and excellence. For by these He has granted to us His precious and magnificent promises, so that by them you may become partakers of the divine nature, having escaped the corruption that is in the world by lust.*

> *I have been crucified with Christ; and it is no longer I who live, but Christ lives in me; and the life which I now live in the flesh I live by faith in the Son of God, who loved me and gave Himself up for me.* Galatians 2:20
>
> *When Christ, who is our life, is revealed, then you also will be revealed with Him in glory.* Colossians 3:4

God gives the new identity to counter our fleshly identity as demonstrated in the following list. What is this new identity in Christ like? Following are a few verses and confessions you can use to begin to understand and appropriate your new identity in Christ (Adapted from <u>The Bondage Breaker</u> by Neil Anderson, Harvest House Publishers, copyright 1990, pages 213–214:

Confess the following truths about yourself…

Because I Am In Christ I Am Secure!

John 1:12	I am a child of God.
Romans 8:1	I am free forever from condemnation.
Romans 8:28–29	I am assured that in all things God will work for my good.
Romans 8:33	I am free from any condemning charges against me.
Romans 8:35	I cannot be separated from the love of Christ.
2 Corinthians 1:21	I have been established, anointed, and sealed by God.
Ephesians 1:13–14	I have been given the Holy Spirit, a pledge, guaranteeing my inheritance to come.
Philippians 4:13	I can do everything through Christ, who gives me strength.
Colossians 1:13	I have been rescued from the dominion of darkness and brought into the kingdom of Christ.
Colossians 3:3	I am hidden with Christ in God.
2 Timothy 1:7	I have not been given a spirit of timidity, but of power, love, and self-discipline.
Hebrews 4:16	I can receive mercy and find grace in time of need.
1 John 5:18	I am born of God and the evil one cannot touch me.

If anyone is in Christ, he is a new creature; the old things passed away; behold, new things have come (2 Cor. 5:17)

Because I Am In Christ I Am Significant!

Matthew 5:13	I am the salt of the earth.
Matthew 5:14	I am the light of the world.
John 1:12	I am God's child.
John 15:5	I am a branch of the true vine, thus a channel of His life.
John 15:16	I have been chosen to bear fruit that will last.
Acts 1:8	I am Christ's personal witness.
1 Corinthians 3:16	I am God's temple.
1 Corinthians 12:27	I am a part of Christ's body.
2 Corinthians 5:18	I am a minister of reconciliation for God.
2 Corinthians 6:1	I am God's fellow worker.
Ephesians 1:1	I am a saint.
Ephesians 2:6	I have been raised up and seated with Christ in heaven.
Philippians 3:20	I am a citizen of heaven.

Because I Am In Christ I Am Accepted!

John 15:15	I am Christ's friend.
Romans 5:1	I have been justified.
1 Corinthians 6:16	I am united with the Lord and I am one with Him in spirit.
1 Corinthians 6:20	I have been bought with a price and belong to God.
1 Corinthians 12:27	I am a part of Christ's body.
2 Corinthians 5:21	I have become righteous.
Ephesians 1:5	I have been adopted as God's child.

Ephesians 2:18	I have direct access to the Father through the Spirit.
Ephesians 2:19	I am a fellow citizen with the rest of the saints.
Ephesians 2:19	I am a member of God's household.
Ephesians 3:12	I may approach God with freedom and confidence.
Colossians 1:14	I have been redeemed and am forgiven of all my sins.
Colossians 2:10	I am complete in Christ.

You will notice that as you read through these new identity truths, your feelings might say, "I don't feel holy," or, "I don't feel like Christ's friend!" This ultimately comes to a faith decision to let go of false beliefs and to instead believe and confess the truth. Realize that your thoughts might run contrary to the truth, and correct them. Emotional idolatry keeps an individual from realizing God's truth in you.

Chapter Eight

The Effect of Belief on Perception

Notice the relational glasses in the diagram? We are going to examine how we see ourselves and others through these glasses. Remember that one lens of the relational glasses comprises negative identity messages you've perceived from imperfect people. It's how you see yourself at your worst. The other lens deals with how you view other individuals at their worst. I will also call these lenses, filters.

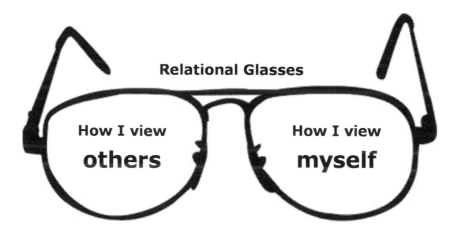

"At my worst, how do I see others, including my spouse?"

Now that we've looked at the personality and flesh, we're turning our attention to the relational glasses. Relationships give meaning and pleasure to life, but they can also create a great source of pain and trouble. Why can relationships cause so much strife?

Have you ever been in a relational situation where it seems you can't do anything right? Maybe the other person viewed most of your words and actions with distrust. If you said, "I love you," or, "I appreciate you," the other responded or thought, "What do you want from me?" If you had said, "I don't like you!" the other could have received that as truth, but when you said, "I appreciate you," the other suspected deception. Why do some of us act that way?

A similar relational dilemma plagued Jesus. Matthew 11:18–19 records the story Jesus told concerning the religious establishment's attitude toward John the Baptist and Jesus's ministries. The religious establishment saw John's lifestyle (restricted eating and drinking habits) and concluded, "He has a demon!" The religious establishment saw Jesus's lifestyle (eating and drinking as any normal Jewish man would) and concluded, "Behold, a gluttonous man and a drunkard!"

The issue was not what John and Jesus did or did not eat or drink. The religious establishment had a belief that those outside of their system couldn't know truth, so no matter what the outsiders did or said, they could not let them in. Jesus and John hadn't jumped through their hoops! Jesus and John hadn't gone to Pharisee or Sadducee seminary. The religious establishment used a filter that invalidated or nullified individuals and their ministries outside the establishment's own training—perhaps in the name of "quality" control (see Mark 6:2–3). As a result, the Pharisees assigned evil motives to what Jesus and John did, viewing them with malice.

In the last several decades, the term "spin doctors" has come to prominence. A spin doctor is one who takes an event, positive or negative, and tries to reinterpret it for the public in self-serving terms. We especially experience this spin in the political arena. It is interesting that Democrats and Republicans can almost always see the same event with such different interpretations.

Yes, to some degree all humans are spin doctors. Part of the problem in relationships is that many believers spin themselves right into divorce court. I don't believe individuals intentionally question their mates' motives, but evidently it does happen. We question each other's motives. We are often told to solve this problem by acting with a "pure motive." Is there such a thing as a pure motive?

Jesus was holy and pure. What He said and did came from the purest of motives. Still, those around Him misinterpreted even His pure words and actions. What makes us think others won't misinterpret what we do or say out of a right motive? What makes us think we won't misinterpret what others do and say? Where do these misinterpretations come from? Everyone has a relational lens that often distorts the message or meaning of another's words and actions.

Some say selfishness or depravity keep individuals from doing anything with a pure motive. They go on to say that if something can't be done with a pure motive, the evil motivation invalidates that action. Let's follow this thinking for a moment. If every motive is tainted with evil, and any decision or action doesn't count because of the evil, then passivity is the only logical action. If you can't do anything right, why do anything at all? Of course, even our passivity is evil!

Whose responsibility is it to reveal the motives of our hearts? These words are recorded in 1 Corinthians 4:5: *Do not go on passing judgment before the time, but wait until the Lord comes who will both bring to light the things hidden in the darkness and disclose the motives of men's hearts; and then each man's praise will come to him from God.*

So what can we do to enable action with a "pure" motive? I've found the quickest way to deal with the motivation problem is to face my own possible motives. I can admit that some of my motives are selfish. But that is the Lord's business: to disclose my motives. I can face a situation and bring all my motives to the Lord and ask what He would have me do. Only the Lord can disclose the motives of our hearts. His ability to reveal what I should do in any case surpasses my ability to discern right motives and act accordingly. Once He reveals His will, then I obey by faith.

What Is a Relational Lens or Filter?

A relational lens is the method through which we read and interpret a relationship, affecting our perception of that relationship, our belief system concerning the relationship. In photography, a colored lens, often called a "filter," distorts the natural color the lens receives and changes the way the picture looks. A red filter placed over the camera lens makes a sunset quite brilliant, transforming the yellow into a bright orange.

When you develop the film, the photo depicts a combination of reality and distortion. The mountains and trees have the same shape and size with or without the red lens filter; only the color distorts. Similarly, a relational filter can distort the way you perceive what others do and say.

The distortion involves elements of truth—the actual words and actions really happened. What comes into question is the interpretation or translation—the color—of those words and actions. The lenses form a part of the relational glasses. The glass or plastic in the lens of a pair of glasses does not physically do anything for the individual's eyes. The lens just distorts (refracts) the light to correct for poor vision caused by the improper shape of the eye.

The other term I've used to describe this perception is "filter." Chemists use a filter to purify or separate out undesirable elements, allowing the desirable elements to pass through or vice versa. Similarly, at times a relational filter only lets negative or positive messages through, resulting in a distortion in our perception of another. When mainly positive messages get through the stage is called infatuation. In an antagonistic relationship, mainly negative messages and actions get through the filter. The point is that once we become aware of our perception we can choose to see the best in others.

What Is the Purpose of a Relational Lens or Filter?

The primary purpose of a relational lens or filter is to allow one individual to perceive another individual. Relational filters are always present because they come from your perceptions—how others might, will, and do respond to you. The question, therefore, is not, "How do I approach a relationship with a blank slate or filter?" but rather, "What types of perceptions have I allowed in my lens or filter?" The beginning point of healing in a relationship involves considering that the perceptions of yourself and others may not be accurate.

How Are Relational Lenses or Filters Developed?

One of the most common influences in the development of the relational filter is hurt. Hurt causes you to develop a protective filter. When you feel hurt by an individual, you respond as if someone were physically hurting you. In order to protect yourself, you might run and hide, or you might fight back (or attack first) to try to prevent the other individual from hurting you. In general we develop either a fight or a flight response when we experience conflict in relationships. How well do the relational lenses or filters work in protecting you from hurt?

When most individuals are asked, "Does the protective filter work?" they respond with "No!" So, does identifying and reprogramming your protective filter insulate you from further hurt? No. Even when we rigidly adhere to a filter, it does not accomplish its purpose. Individuals are not perfect and do appear to hurt one another continually. Hurt is a normal part of a relationship. Since the protective filter has its roots in hurt, a person naturally responds to additional hurt by raising the protective filter up once again, reinstating the belief, "I should never have trusted that person again or allowed myself to be vulnerable."

The result belief leads us to isolate ourselves from the very thing we so desperately need: an intimate, loving, healthy relationship.

How Can I Identify My Relational Lens or Filter?

Perhaps the easiest way to identify this filter is to do the following exercise. Check the characteristics that describe your view of your most significant relationship at its worst moment. This how you feel they are like during conflict. This exercise will help you discover feelings and trace those feelings back to a belief system.

I feel that this person is:

☐abusive ☐against me ☐always right ☐angry
☐cheating on me ☐controlling ☐defensive ☐demanding
☐disappointed ☐emotional ☐explosive ☐harsh
☐hard to please ☐impersonal ☐incapable ☐inconsistent
☐inconsiderate ☐irrational ☐irresponsible ☐insecure
☐insensitive ☐manipulative ☐moody ☐quiet
☐trying to change me ☐selfish ☐rejecting me ☐unforgiving
☐unaffectionate ☐uncomplimentary
☐unkind ☐unloving ☐unrealistic ☐untrustworthy
☐withdrawn ☐will disappoint me

These lenses of our relational glasses distort the messages received in relationships. Let's suppose your spouse or fiancé comes to you and says, by God's direction in pure motive, "I love you!" with no conditions attached. Let's also suppose you are very angry. What possible motive distortions could the emotional relational lens make of the words, "I love you"?

If a woman feels all males are untrustworthy, she interprets his assertion as, "He's just trying to manipulate me!" or thinks, "I wonder what he wants?" or "What has he done?" or "He's lying!" The woman responds with malice, attributing an evil motive to his words due to her basic emotional beliefs about males.

Jesus had to deal with malice regarding the Pharisees in Matthew 22:15, 18: *The Pharisees went and plotted together how they might trap Him in what He said. But Jesus perceived their malice, and said, "Why are you testing Me, you hypocrites?"* The Pharisees wanted to take Jesus's answer to their questions and use it against Him.

Notice that the relational lenses are connected by a nose piece. There is a connection between how others can seem at their worst and how you see yourself at your worst. While counseling couples, I've noticed that when they come in angry, they immediately argue to "prove" something. Generally, proof includes a history lesson: "Remember when you…?" Whatever the issue—money, sex, kids—it is used to prove just how inadequate the spouse really is. The question is, what's the point? What does one accomplish by proving how rotten the other person is?

Here's what it proves. It proves we really are unloved, or neglected, or stupid. You see, the harder we try to prove how bad our spouse is, the more proof we provide about how bad we are. We throw mud on our spouse and we get dirty. That sounds like oneness to me! In summary, tearing our spouse apart (or ourselves for that matter) goes nowhere.

Chapter Nine

Changing My Relational Filter?

Once you begin to identify and change your relational filter (glasses lens), you might see your spouse or friend get rather uncomfortable and start to push your "buttons" to try to get you to respond like you've always done in the past. He or she consciously or unconsciously tries to recreate the former relational patterns. Change on your part will necessitate change on his or her part if he or she wants to continue to relate to you. Therefore, your change makes the other person uncomfortable.

What can you do with this protective lens or filter? What steps can you take to identify and remove the relational glasses?

1. Ask God to help you identify the elements in your relational glasses. You already did this when you checked the emotions in the previous chapter's lists. If you haven't yet, take a few minutes to fill those out.

2. Evaluate the elements of your lens in light of Scripture and your new identity in Christ. Confess the new identity truths about yourself! These can be found in previous chapters.

3. Confess as sin those elements you've used to protect yourself that keep you from relating with others the way God intended. You can generally see selfish motivation involved in a sinful style of protection.

4. Forgive others for the hurt you feel they caused you. Unforgiveness can allow others to continue to hurt us. Why? Unforgiveness is unfinished business in our relationships with others.

5. Confess God as your Protector. Why? Looking to and trusting something other than the Lord for protection is idolatry. Yes, your protective lens can become an idol. *Let him rely on My protection, Let him make peace with Me* (Isa. 27:5).

6. Face the fear of becoming vulnerable and getting hurt again. As we have close relationships with others we will have misunderstandings. Misunderstandings are normal.

7. Commit yourself to the union, trusting God to create a new and different relationship.

8. Trust Him to work out the details.

9. Treat your spouse according to his or her new identity in Christ.

Once you realize your relational glasses are faulty, you can identify and reprogram the lens by faith. Reprogramming, in essence, has been done by the Lord. He gives the only sane estimate of yourself and others.

Faith at work means accepting God's perception of others, not relying on your own perceptions. Ask Him to reveal how He sees people. In the marriage relationship, ask God to love your spouse through you, giving you the desire and strength to do His will. In and of ourselves, it is not possible to love as He loved. Only He can do that, and He lives in us.

Chapter Ten

The Relational Furnace

There comes a crossroads in most marriages where a decision has to be made, a decision the couple typically thought they had already made: "We made the decision to stay in the marriage! Divorce is not an option!" Though the couple made those vows, some eventually come to a point where they ask, "Will we stay in the marriage, or will we get out and try it with someone else?" What leads married believers to this point?

Day-in and day-out conflict, heartache, and arguing wear them down. "This marriage is only making us more and more miserable." They heard marriage brings out the best and worst in you—well, they wonder, where's the best? They can only see the worst. They get tired of marriage misery. Was marriage designed to make you miserable? Is this misery normal? The answer might surprise you—yes! Let's look more closely at the process of marriage and God's plan to create marriages that glorify Him.

The Marriage Process

The first seven years in a typical marriage involve the following:

- Discovering the strengths and weaknesses of yourself and your spouse
- Discovering a faith-based love for your spouse
- Becoming increasingly irritated with your spouse's weaknesses

- Failing when trying to smooth over conflicts
- Trying to get your spouse to meet your needs, emotional, sexual, and otherwise
- Trying to make your spouse see and do things your way

Essentially, you are trying to change your spouse into what you think will meet your needs.

In marriage, eventually his flesh will aggravate her flesh, and her flesh will aggravate his flesh, and they will become more and more miserable. The couple shares in the suffering caused by fleshly selfish living. What is God's plan for selfish flesh? Galatians 5:17 reads, *For the flesh sets its desire against the Spirit, and the Spirit against the flesh; for these are in opposition to one another, so that you may not do the things that you please.*

The Spirit sets against the flesh and a battle occurs. Marriage can be viewed as God's perfect plan designed to bring to the surface the self-life in both the husband and wife so the Lord can heal what is revealed.

The ultimate goal of the journey to the end of a fleshly marriage is a new beginning in a precious, Christ-centered, God-glorifying, and, most importantly, oneness relationship. A certain stop along the way can be very unpleasant. The couple realizes the marriage, as they know it, is in serious trouble. They come to realize a miracle holds their only hope for keeping the relationship together. They, despite their most valiant efforts, cannot put it back together without God. What does God's marriage-purifying process look like?

The Purifying Process

Proverbs 25:4 describes the overall goal of purification, using the illustration of producing a silver vessel: *Take away the dross from the silver, and there comes out a vessel for the smith.*

Years ago my wife and I went to Williamsburg, Virginia, to the refurbished colonial village. We watched a silversmith working in his shop. The process of making a silver vessel goes something like this: First, the smith places raw silver ore in an extremely hot furnace to melt it. The silver sinks to the bottom, while the dross (impurities made up of dirt and other materials) floats to the top. The smith then pours the dross off, leaving the silver in the container.

Next, the smith forms the molten silver by pouring it into a mold for a vessel. After the metal cools and hardens, the smith takes it out of the mold and works on the vessel. He taps, etches, and polishes the vessel until it is finished and ready for use.

So why talk about the making of silver vessels in regards to marriage relationships? Most marriages God works through will experience those stages: separation of the dross from the silver, pouring the silver in a mold, taking the vessel out of the mold and polishing, and finally, becoming ready for use.

Sadly, many marriages never make it through the first step—separating the precious silver (spirit) from the worthless dross (flesh). The following diagram describes this process. Eventually the couple comes to a crossroads in their marriage, entering the most intense purification time of their relationship. They must make a decision to allow God's purification or to cut and run.

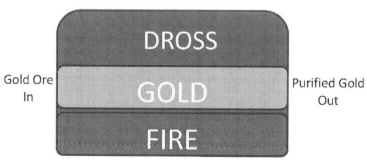

Relational Purifying Furnace

The Crossroads

At the crossroads, or door of the furnace, the couple or individual contemplates whether or not the marriage will continue. This contemplation is *normal.* The couple reaches what they perceive as a dead end, the door of the marriage furnace. Most resist coming to the door of the furnace because they consider the marriage furnace abnormal.

Remember, they made a commitment to stay married to each other and now they can't stand each other! This resistance retards the normal marriage maturation process. No one likes the furnace, but the furnace is necessary to burn the dross away from a fleshly marriage so a precious, Christ-centered, God-glorifying marriage can result. So what happens in the purifying marriage furnace?

The Purifying Furnace

In the furnace the heat gets turned up, and the emotional love for each other seems to turn off. Keep in mind that the Lord is producing the Christ-centered marriage He intended all along. At this time He reveals just how much flesh has been involved in driving the marriage. To reveal this fleshly work, He allows the exposure of what needs healing in the marriage. The couple is finally hit with the reality that *apart from Him we can do nothing* (John 15:5), including stay married.

During this fiery ordeal, the Lord seeks to reestablish the marriage on a new basis and life source—Christ's life. How long does this furnace experience last? That's the Lord's business, but practically speaking, the answer is, "as long as it takes." Resisting His working in your life and marriage prolongs the process.

Some are not willing to live another day in their current condition, so they opt for another spouse. When they opt for another, they go back to the beginning and get in line for His process to begin again, which eventually leads them back to the door of the furnace. Some repeat the process over and over again while shortening the time from the wedding to the furnace. When the couple reaches the door of the furnace, they believe staying married will result in death. They mistakenly define their predicament as time to divorce instead of time for death of the self and rebirth in Christ.

Let's look at the lives of some individuals who actually experienced the furnace. The story begins when King Nebuchadnezzar orders all his kingdom to worship a gold image. Daniel, Shadrach, Meshach, and Abed-nego were Jews who had been exiled in the kingdom. They would not bow and worship the golden image. This story is recorded in Daniel 3:19–30: *Nebuchadnezzar was filled with wrath, and his facial expression was altered toward Shadrach, Meshach, and Abed-nego. He answered by giving orders to heat the furnace seven times more than it was usually heated. And he commanded certain valiant warriors who were in his army to tie up Shadrach, Meshach, and Abed-nego, in order to cast them into the furnace of blazing fire. Then these men were tied up in their trousers, their coats, their caps, and their other clothes, and were cast into the midst of the furnace of blazing fire. For this reason, because the king's command was urgent and the furnace had been made extremely hot, the flame of the fire slew those men who carried up Shadrach, Meshach, and Abed-nego. But these three men, Shadrach, Meshach, and Abed-nego, fell into the midst of the furnace of blazing fire still tied up.*

Then Nebuchadnezzar the king was astounded and stood up in haste; he responded and said to his high officials, "Was it not three men we cast bound into the midst of the fire?" They answered and said to the king, "Certainly, O king." He answered and said, "Look! I see four men loosed and walking about in the midst of the fire without harm, and the appearance of the fourth is like a son of the gods!" Then Nebuchadnezzar came near to the door of the furnace of blazing fire; he responded and said, "Shadrach, Meshach, and Abed-nego, come out, you servants of the Most High God, and come here." Then Shadrach, Meshach, and Abed-nego came out of the midst of the fire. And the satraps, the prefects, the governors and the king's high officials gathered around and saw in regard to these men that the fire had no effect on the bodies of these men nor was the hair of their head singed, nor were their trousers damaged, nor had the smell of fire even come upon them.

Do you think the king asked Shadrach, Meshach, and Abed-nego to come out of the fire because he cared about them personally? No, he was interested in that fourth man he'd described as "like a son of the gods!"

You see, as you walk by faith in what God has led you to in your commitment to each other, you will at some point come to a place of saying, as in Daniel 3:17, *Our God whom we serve is able to deliver us from the furnace of blazing fire.*

You will come to a point when you realize only God can put your relationship back together again. What will the result be? People will want to meet your "fourth man," and they will note that a miracle has indeed taken place. Who will get the credit? Shadrach, Meshach, and Abed-nego did not take the glory—that belongs solely to the Lord God—and neither can the couple the Lord brings through the furnace.

Notice the response of King Nebuchadnezzar and who received the glory for this miracle in Daniel 3:28–29: *Nebuchadnezzar responded and said, "Blessed be the God of Shadrach, Meshach, and Abed-nego, who has sent His angel and delivered His servants who put their trust in Him, violating the king's command, and yielded up their bodies so as not to serve or worship any god except their own God. Therefore, I make a decree that any people, nation, or tongue that speaks anything offensive against the God of Shadrach, Meshach, and Abed-nego shall be torn limb from limb and their houses reduced to a rubbish heap, inasmuch as there is no other god who is able to deliver in this way."*

The Lord will bring you through the fire, just as He did Shadrach, Meshach, and Abed-nego. Trust in Him. These three men didn't trust in their own ability to withstand heat—they were brought through by the Lord. At this crisis point some say, "I don't feel like continuing on in this marriage!"

I often ask, "Do you always feel like going to work?"

They say "No!"

"So, why do you go to work then?" I ask.

"I want to get paid! I've got to go to work in order to live!"

Why is this marriage decision any different? Do you want the payoff, a Christ-centered marriage? Do you want a marriage that expresses oneness with your spouse? The process takes time. It often takes years to get to this particular point in a relationship, and it will take time to build a new marriage based on the truths of God's Word.

In the process of emotional separation, a man and woman, through conflicts, misunderstanding, and disagreements, slowly move away from each other emotionally. Through time they make many decisions to move away from the other individual. Often these decisions are motivated by feelings, by believing the worst of the other person.

Eventually, husband and wife view each other with malice. They think and believe the worst of each other. This is the point where a faith decision must be made so the relationship can heal. The road back to healing involves a number of faith decisions to move toward the other individual.

The faith steps made toward healing are motivated by faith and obedience. These steps involve believing the best in your partner. Healing the marriage requires the promotion of oneness. Just as it took time to create emotional separation, it will take time to create emotional closeness. Take the time to put aside the blame of the past, forgiving old pain and hurt.

How Do You Know When You Are in the Marriage Furnace?

The following survey contains possible indications that you are in the marriage furnace or at its door. Rank yourself and your spouse in the following survey on a scale from one to ten, in which one means rarely, and ten means always.

You/Spouse

☐ ☐ Emotional coldness toward the other

☐ ☐ Lack of compassion toward the other

☐ ☐ Focusing on what's wrong in the relationship

☐ ☐ List keeping of wrongdoings to rationalize emotional desire for divorce

☐ ☐ Lack of forgiveness

☐ ☐ Constant disunity in relationship

☐ ☐ Seeking affirmations of love in other relationships or friendships

☐ ☐ Unwilling to admit mistakes, much less take responsibility

☐ ☐ Waiting for the other to repent before you do ("You go first!")

☐ ☐ Trying to escape from relating, through job, work, television, books, children

☐ ☐ Trying to persuade others just how bad you have it

☐ ☐ Pulling away from the Lord; after all, look what He did to you ("Why didn't He protect me?")

☐ ☐ Fear that your repentance will result in strengthening spouse's position

☐ ☐ Expecting your spouse to change even though you won't change yourself

☐ ☐ Open hostility toward the other

☐ ☐ Passive-style aggression toward the other (cold-shouldering, for example)

☐ ☐ Hiding money or resources from spouse, for when "it" happens

☐ ☐ Feelings of bitterness toward spouse

☐ ☐ Holding spouse to a higher standard than you're willing to live up to

☐ ☐ Giving or taking too much responsibility for the relationship

☐ ☐ Unwillingness to communicate

Can I Enter the Furnace Alone if My Spouse Is Unwilling to Do Anything?

There is plenty of work to do individually and as a couple. Remember that this process takes time. You can allow the Lord to do what He needs to do in your life regardless of whether your spouse is with you.

The journey to the end of a fleshly marriage runs parallel to the journey to the end of self. Married or single, the Lord in His faithfulness and compassion will take you to the end of your fleshly self—the end of your trusting in idols, the end of your trusting in your own strength and wisdom, the end of your trusting in man's provision.

The journey may be lonesome, and often you will miss the intimacy of sharing your experiences with another, unless you have a good friend (preferably same-sex) to share with. As you go through the process, remember that your spouse might or might not respond.

If separated, the roving spouse might attempt to come back "if you keep your act together." Often he can see a newfound sense of peace in your life due to the changes the Lord has made in your attitude and behavior. It is essential that both spouses come to the place where they will do anything the Lord desires in putting their relationship back together.

How Will My Spouse Respond to Me if I Change?

Most spouses respond to change in the other by "button pushing." Button pushing involves someone intentionally doing or saying things in order to irritate you, hopefully to the point where you lose your cool! This person is fishing for a reaction.

Expect the spouse, who either isn't aware of or is unwilling to consider what the Lord is doing, to try to keep the old relationship dynamic looping. Your spouse may do so even if the new you is much better than the old you. You can expect your changes to make your spouse uncomfortable. Your spouse knows at a core level that change means he or she needs to change in order to relate to you, your spouse will be challenged to evaluate his or her own selfishness, or both.

Change is uncomfortable, so your spouse will try harder and harder to get you to fail (and you will fail!). I am not promoting failure here but setting the stage for when failure does occur. To expect perfection in your words and actions is somewhat unrealistic. What's most important is how you respond to challenges—will you give up and go back to the old you, or will you commit your ways to the Lord and walk on with Him? Your spouse will learn more from your response to the Lord than from your words about how much you've changed.

The spouse who sees the marriage furnace in action tends to push the mate into the furnace, exhibiting a "you first" mentality ("Let's see if this thing really works. If you're not destroyed, then I'll follow you in.") The faith response, regardless of your mate's response, is to walk into the furnace by faith.

What do I mean by pushing your mate into the furnace? Nagging; being contrary; fighting; picking on your mate; being moody, angry, or bitter; all in all, just plain being self-centered. "Let's see how my spouse can handle this!" This is just an excuse to feed your flesh! You are purposely making life hell for your mate. Remember that just because you see your mate in misery, it doesn't necessarily mean that you're doing something wrong. Righteous living can also make your mate's life a living hell.

A pastor once told me the two main reasons pastors are asked to leave the church are flagrant sin and flagrant righteousness. Jesus was crucified because of His righteousness. It is good to suffer for righteousness' sake (see 1 Pet. 3:14).

Can you now see that the Lord allows marital suffering to bring the believer face to face with the self the believer must deny and to reveal the purpose of the Cross? Only as we abide in the Lord can we ever experience the joy He provides (see Gal. 5:22–23). We learn that joy comes not from our circumstances, or how well our spouse meets our needs, but from His life in us (see Col. 3:4).

Yes, we can come to a point of appreciation for the conflict and suffering in our marriage when we see His provision through it all and experience the change He brings to us through His life within. Only when we give up trying to save our marriage ourselves will we allow the Lord to save our marriage. Only when we realize "we can't" will we understand that He can! Give your marriage to Him, but first give yourself to Him.

What Does a Christ-Centered Marriage Look Like?

Tension occurs when one tries to change the other into what that person wants, or even what God wants. As a couple, you might see and understand what God wants in your relationship with each other.

The question then becomes, how do we get from where we are to where God wants us to be? How can we grow from a fleshly relationship to a Christ-centered relationship? The following table contrasts the fleshly way of trying to change a spouse vs. the Christ-centered way of drawing out the best in a spouse.

The following compares a Christ-centered marriage in contrast to the fleshly marriage. Which ways have you tried? Which method do you identify with most? Has it worked?

Christ-Centered Marriage versus Fleshly Marriage

Emphasis in trusting the Lord with your mate's needs	Emphasis on your mate's ability to meet your needs
Failure seen as an opportunity to grow	Failure seen as another step to the end
Conflict as an area in which to trust God	Conflict as another stamp in the "bitter book"
Says: "Let's draw nearer in order to be a better spouse."	Says: "If you improve (be a better spouse), then I'll let you near."
Appreciation of your mate's differences	Attempt to stamp out your mate's differences
Desire to understand the spouse and hear him or her	Only desire to be understood and to speak
Draw the best out of mate through forgiveness, grace, and love	Motivate spouse to change by using guilt andconflict

Give mate the benefit of the
doubt in actions and words

Attribute evil motives to mate's
actions and words

In summary:
- All couples have strengths and weaknesses (flesh and Spirit)
- The Lord uses relationships to bring out these strengths and weaknesses
- Conflict within a relationship is normal
- Fleshly responses to conflict promote separation
- Faith responses promote a oneness

How can we allow God to heal our relationship once it has been devastated by years of bickering and fighting? It is very helpful to have some steps to use as a guide to allowing the Lord to heal the relationship.

Chapter Eleven

Allowing God to Heal Your Marriage

The following steps are designed to help a couple begin the journey back to a healthy Christ-centered relationship. The steps will sometimes (or often) seem impossible. The first four basic steps build a foundation for the following steps.

These helpful steps allow the Lord to help you on your way to a whole marriage:

1. Make sure you are a born-again believer. If you don't know what this means, ask your pastor or some growing believers.

2. Seek to allow Christ to be the Lord and only boss of your life.

3. Accept God's view of you, ask God to reveal how He views you. As a new creation in Christ, you have a new identity.

4. Walk in Christ as your very life, day by day and moment by moment.

5. Give and receive forgiveness from your spouse, through confession and repentance.

6. Do the homework God reveals or that is assigned to you by a pastor or counselor. The key here is that you bring your relationship before the Lord in prayer and ask God to show you what He has in mind for you and your spouse.

7. Trust in Him for leadership and guidance by seeking Him each day.

8. Change ways of communicating with your spouse to ensure that both of you benefit and neither speaks in accordance with relational glasses or false perceptions.

9. Give grace and be compassionate to your spouse, and have patience for his or her personal challenges as well as your own personal changes.

10. Work out new marriage vows allowing God to build a "new" union between you and your spouse.

11. Remember to promote unity and oneness in the relationship. Identify attitudes and behaviors that promote oneness. Identify and confess attitudes and behaviors that promote disharmony.

12. Sign the commitment form below, and allow your pastor, counselor, or accountability marriage watcher to review your commitments.

I desire to seek Him and His plan for my life and relationship.

Date:

Name:

Witnessed by:

You might not understand all the ramifications of each of the above steps, and you must therefore walk day by day in faith that the Lord has taken control. It is often difficult to make this commitment, and many individuals sign and use this as a guide.

Chapter Twelve

Communication through Difficulties

How Can We See Our Way through Conflict?

Conflict inevitably occurs in any growing relationship. In fact, any relationship continually cycles through two elements: alienation and reconciliation. When experiencing alienation, we disagree or misunderstand. As we work through the difficulty, we come to a place of understanding and, therefore, reconciliation.

During conflict it is important to remember that your spouse isn't the enemy. Attack the problem instead of each other. How can a couple desiring to allow God to heal their marriage deal with conflict that invariably comes up?

The following questions are designed for use after you and your mate have discovered your flesh patterns. Use the following questions to work your way through conflicts that arise day by day:

1. What seems to be the issue we disagree on? What's the *real* issue? What outcome do I desire? What outcome do you desire?

2. Which relational lens elements could possibly be affecting our views of the issue and each other? What could I or you be communicating unintentionally?

3. How could we respectfully communicate with each other in such a way that promotes understanding?

4. How could I state my perspective differently so that it will not seem negative or like an attack on you?

5. What do you think I intend in looking at the issue the way I do? What do you intend in perceiving the issue the way you do?

6. What is the issue in view of your most basic desires—in your relationship to God, your spouse, to the kids, etc.?

A Communication Method

Years ago I read US Army Colonel Henry Martyn Robert's *Pocket Manual of Rules of Order for Deliberative Assemblies*, published in February 1876. *Robert's Rules of Order*, as it's known, provides a means for my church to discuss various problems and decisions in an orderly fashion.

In the same way, couples need "rules of order" to facilitate healthy communication with each other. Sadly, many couples have never learned how to have a conversation with each other in the midst of conflict. Below I have provided a method for communicating with someone during a disagreement or misunderstanding.

Communication during conflict requires that the couple seek to understand each other. While one individual talks, the other should listen. This might seem very simplistic, but I have been amazed at how many couples cannot (or will not) seek to understand the other.

Couples need a basic, orderly method of communication that allows a couple to speak and be heard, a sort of *Robert's Rules of Order* for couple-dom. In the following method, one shares while the other listens until the one speaking senses that the other understands (not necessarily agrees). The sharer and listener then change roles. The following rules will help ensure an orderly way of communicating:

Rules for the One Talking

1. Share your own feelings and perspective on the disagreement or misunderstanding. Try not to put words in the other's mouth and don't assume you know what the other meant by his or her words or actions. Share an event the way you saw it unfold and say what you were feeling in the midst of the event.

2. Shorten the talk, keeping it brief because your spouse will need to summarize what you say. Start with something like, "I felt like…" and make sure he or she understands you (not necessarily agrees with you) before going on to another point.

3. Stop after explaining your feelings and perception. The pause gives your spouse time to paraphrase what you've said so you can be sure you two are on the same page (or somewhere in the vicinity).

Rules for the One Trying to Understand

1. Listen to what your spouse is saying and pay attention to his or her demeanor. Put all selfish thoughts and feelings away to concentrate on understanding what the other is saying. It can be helpful to take notes.

2. Summarize what you hear the other saying. Be careful not to interject your own perspective or feelings. Your goal is to understand their view of the situation. "So I hear you saying…"

3. Affirm what the other person is saying, for example "I can see why you feel that way!" or "I understand why you did that."

Rules for Both to Remember

1. Wait for the person sharing to finish.

2. Allow the summarizer to finish summarizing.

3. Ask questions to clarify. ("I really don't know what you meant when you said you felt abandoned. Could you please describe that feeling?")

While communicating, it is important to look for what you or your spouse really wants to glean from the other. For example, during one conversation a husband wanted his spouse to value his leadership and decisions while the wife wanted to know of his love and care for her. The harder the husband tried to explain how disrespected or dishonored he felt, the more the wife felt like an unlovable failure. Unwittingly, they became their own worst enemies in terms of communication. Remember that a spouse cannot meet the need for perfect love and acceptance that only God can give. When we look to our spouse to meet needs only God can meet, we will be disappointed. In doing so we live with unrealistic expectations that continually go unmet. The following are some common "agendas," expectations, or affirmations we commonly look for during communication.

Common Communication Agendas

1. Control

Many issues in a relationship deal with control. Who takes charge or who makes the decisions about where we go or what we do, or how we spend the money or raise the kids? Control-oriented people tend to get a sense of importance and security from being in charge. If not in control they feel less than or less important than another individual.

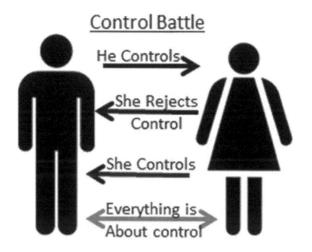

In the battle for control, the controller becomes the controlled. They swap roles in the relationship, and in this case she becomes the very thing she disliked. Making a decision becomes difficult because it is not about the decision but about control. The real question becomes obscured. What do You want us to do, Lord? If you find yourself in the control battle, learn to respect each other, treat each other accordingly, and seek what God would have you do.

2. Trust

When trust becomes an agenda, the individual questions the other's integrity. Is his word good or dependable? Does she really believe what she professes? Often one person examines the other's behavior closely to determine whether that behavior is genuine.

3. Commitment

Commitment as an agenda pushes some individuals to place their spouses in situations that force them to choose between friends, churches, television programs, family, and more. "If you really love me and are committed to me you won't go out with your friends anymore."

4. Love

The individual who uses love as an agenda will ask questions like, "Do you really love me? Will you still love me if I fail? Are you really concerned with me and my life?"

5. Respect

When respect becomes an agenda, the individual asks questions like, "Do you respect me? Do you respect my thoughts and feelings? Why don't you treat me with respect? You don't seem to listen to or value what I'm saying."

You're Not Finished Yet!

You might have some understanding of your spouse's feelings and perceptions, and you might have even identified some of the basic agendas in communication. Now that you have gained a little understanding, it is important to take the next step.

Determine Heart Issues

Here's a simple way to get to heart issues. Heart issues are those issues that resonate deeply within your soul. Think back over what the other said and what they revealed about their heart.

What is the other's heart saying?

What does the other really want?

What legitimate yearning lies behind the words?

For example, when someone says, "I don't feel that you include me in your plans and your life," that person may feel under valued or disrespected. Is there anything wrong with wanting to be valued, loved, respected, or included? No, those are legitimate wants, but they do not come on demand. Love and respect demanded never satisfy.

In the example above, one would make a list of what the other could possibly want:

I want to be loved.

I want to be accepted.

I want to be valued.

I want to be included.

I want to be special.

I want to be secure.

I want to be preferred.

I want to be a priority.

I want to be trusted.

I want to be honored.

Rank the preceding descriptors as to how they resonate to your heart and spirit.

What are your top three desires?

Let's say that the following desires resonate: I want to be a priority, loved, and trusted. Those three resonated when I considered what my heart wanted. Have both members of the couple do the same exercise to determine the top three desires. Write them down. The next time you practice the communication exercise, start out by stating your basic heart desires. You may find that starting there will help to get you further along in communication.

Another Communication Misunderstanding: Definitions

A common cause of misunderstanding deals with definitions. We often do not take the time to understand how the other defines certain aspects of life. It is like we have a life dictionary in our heads that contains words defined through life experiences. Suppose the wife says, "Let's clean the house." In the husband's life-experience dictionary, clean means "a pathway to the door." In the wife's life-experience dictionary, clean means "immaculate." Can you see how a misunderstanding might occur?

The conversation may go like this:

Wife: Why didn't you clean the living room?

Husband: I did clean it!

Wife: No, you didn't; it's a mess!

Husband: There is a pathway to the door, isn't there?

We need to define many words as we relate. Some of these words are love, clean, vacation, cook, faith, sacrifice, work, study, fun, and the list goes on. Years ago my wife and I went someplace special for our first anniversary. We learned that we had different definitions of vacation. She defined vacation as a "change of activity." Instead of being busy at home, she wanted to be busy on vacation. There were plenty of things to do, places to go, places to shop, typical activities for travelers. My definition of vacation was "a cessation of activity." I preferred to sleep in, read a book around the pool, nap, eat, nap again, typical activities for weary travelers. Some relational problems have roots in misunderstanding another's perception or definition. We have since planned to do both types of activities during a vacation, which has made vacations much more pleasant.

We are all just beginning the journey into relationship. We will have eternity to learn about relationships, do relationships, and experience relationships. I still often sense I've only scratched the surface of the relational maze.

May the Lord guide you as you seek to live in a way pleasing to Him. May the Lord lead you into the relationships He has planned for you. Remember that His ability to lead you into deeply satisfying relationships is much greater than your ability to produce one on your own. Give Him a chance to do His work. Trust Him.

John 15:5 reads, *"I am the vine, you are the branches; he who abides in Me and I in him, he bears much fruit, for apart from Me you can do nothing."*

About the Author

Scott Hadden was born in 1952 in a little town in Northwest Iowa. He attended Iowa State University and the University of Nebraska, receiving his BS and MS degrees, and earned his DPhil in counseling at Oxford Graduate School. He went into full-time ministry in 1979, working on university campuses and ministries in Iowa, Nebraska, Kansas, Oklahoma, Colorado, Texas, and Zambia, Africa. He was director of training for Abiding Life Ministries Internataional, Grace Fellowship International and for Scope Ministries International. He and his wife, Pam, live in Edmond, Oklahoma where he is president of Scope Ministries International in Oklahoma City. They have two sons and three grandsons.

41084554R00070

Made in the USA
Charleston, SC
18 April 2015